TRAVELLERS

ARGENTINA

By
JANE EGGINTON AND IAIN MACINTYRE

Written by Jane Egginton and Iain MacIntyre

Original photography by Jane Egginton and Iain MacIntyre

Editing and page layout by Cambridge Publishing Management Ltd,
Unit 2, Burr Elm Court, Caldecote CB23 7NU
Series Editor: Karen Beaulah

Published by Thomas Cook Publishing
A division of Thomas Cook Tour Operations Ltd
Company Registration No. 1450464 England

PO Box 227, The Thomas Cook Business Park,
Coningsby Road, Peterborough PE3 8SB, United Kingdom
E-mail: books@thomascook.com
www.thomascookpublishing.com
Tel: +44 (0)1733 416477

ISBN: 978-1-84157-809-5

Project Editor: Linda Bass
Production/DTP Editor: Steven Collins

Printed and bound in Italy by: Printer Trento.

Contents

Background   **4–21**
Introduction   4
The land   8
History   10
Politics   14
Culture   16
Festivals and events   20

Highlights   **22–5**
Highlights   22
Suggested itineraries   24

Destination guide   **26–119**
Buenos Aires   26
Central and Southern Patagonia   48
Tierra del Fuego   66
The Lake District   76
Mendoza and wine country   90
Córdoba and the Central Sierras   100
Salta and surrounds   110

Getting away from it all   **120–25**

Practical guide   **126–59**
When to go   126
Getting around   128
Accommodation   132
Food and drink   136
Entertainment   140
Shopping   142
Sport and leisure   144
Children   148
Essentials   150
Language   156
Emergencies   158

Directory   **160–72**

Index   **173–5**

Maps
Argentina   6–7
Highlights   22
Buenos Aires   26
Buenos Aires, city   27
Central and Southern Patagonia   48
Tour: Península Valdés   52
Tierra del Fuego   66
The Lake District   76
Tour: Manso River adventure   84
Mendoza and wine country   90
Tour: A wine route   94
Córdoba and the Central Sierras   100
Tour: A hillside drive   109
Salta and surrounds   110
Tour: Quebrada de Humahuaca   116

Features
Indigenous people   18
Maradona   36
Los Gauchos   42
Patagonian wildlife   56
Explorers – Darwin and Moreno   72
Activities in the Lake District   88
Fine Argentine wine   96
Argentina's master crafts   118
Estancias   134

Tours
Iguazú Falls and Parque Nacional
    Iguazú   46
Península Valdés   52
Voyage at the end of the earth   70
Manso River adventure   84
A wine route   94
A hillside drive   108
Changing plains – south of
    the city   114
Quebrada de Humahuaca   116

Introduction

All the way down in the south of South America is a land of gauchos with their lyrical songs, legendary steaks, Patagonian plains and, at the end of the earth, Tierra del Fuego – the evocative land of fire that leads to the ice continent of Antarctica. In an all-too-crowded world, Argentina ignites the imagination and has an almost magnetic pull. The wide-open expanses of Patagonia, the endless pampas *(large plains) and the mammoth Andean mountain range sit beneath enormous, cloudless skies, dwarfing their visitors with a spine-tingling perspective on nature's expanse.*

There are unforgettable close-ups, too, like the flip of the tail of a great whale, the braying cacophony of penguins, and watering the horses after a long day's ride. The Perito Moreno glacier is a living, breathing colossus, noisily shedding boat-sized pieces of ice, yet composed enough to let you tread its surface. The waterfalls of Iguazú thunder with the force of an ocean, spraying the faces of eager onlookers. These dynamic giants are all the more awe-inspiring for their accessibility.

In Argentina, it is easy to feel at home. Buenos Aires (often referred to as BA), with its cultivated parks and bookish population, is a decidedly urbane, almost Parisian capital. The culture shock that immediately hits the visitor in other Latin American cities is absent here. It is easy to get into the swing of this country, whether in the capital's café society, or in the nearby rural splendour of the *estancias*

(ranches) with their old-fashioned welcomes. As one estancia owner put it: 'We have everything here: wonderful people, beautiful landscapes and world-class wine…'

The same woman went on to say that 'the only thing we don't have is decent politicians.' Argentina's modern past has not been a happy one. The scars of military dictatorship and 'the disappeared' run deep. The recent economic crisis, when the currency was drastically devalued, hit everyone hard. Blinkered mismanagement, greed and corruption are endemic within politics and big business. Visitors will sense this, in the rampant exploitation of certain natural wonders, and in higher 'tourist prices' they are charged for hotels and internal flights. Yet Argentina offers many memorable journeys; some are on well-trodden paths, others along isolated, little-travelled roads. In the north, traditional

Horse riding through the forest

trading routes take the visitor from historic colonial towns, past the remains of Inca settlements, and to sleepy villages nestled in dramatic multicoloured ravines. Close to Córdoba, a scenic circuit links a network of historic Jesuit estancias, built to feed the priests and the natives they were trying to 'civilise'. Mendoza has the popular and indulgent Wine Route, which takes the visitor from one welcoming *bodega* (winery) to another.

Ruta 40, running all the way from the Lake District to the southern tip of the country, is a three-day 'road trip' through a wilderness that is remote even by Patagonia's standards. Throughout Argentina, there is always the chance to get off the beaten track, where even the locals are constantly discovering something new in this country the size of a continent.

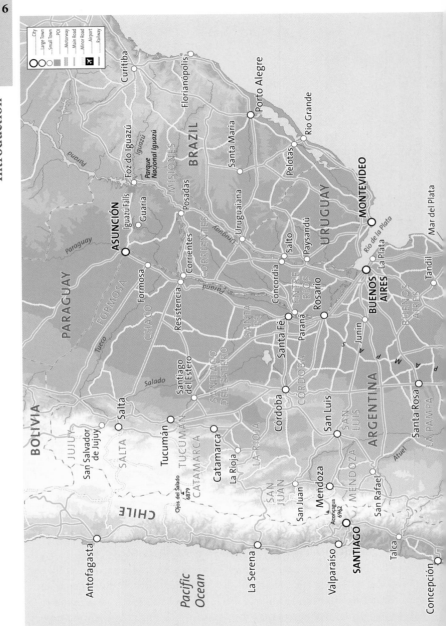

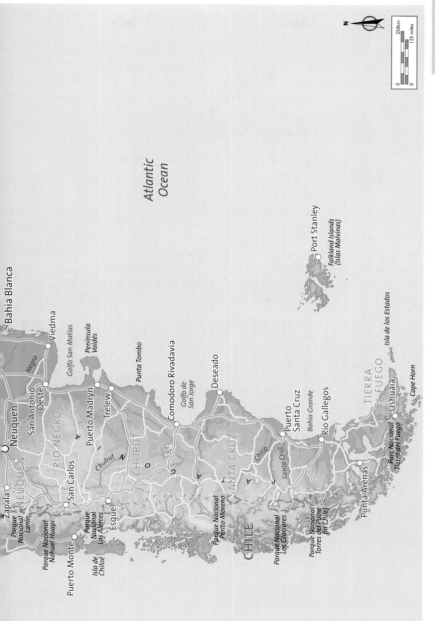

The land

Argentina, the enormous elephant trunk of land that forms the southern cone of South America, stretches for a staggering 3,500km (2,175 miles) from its northern border with Bolivia to the southern tip of Tierra del Fuego. This is the eighth largest country in the world; the province of Buenos Aires alone is the size of France.

Argentina has it all in terms of geography, from semi-tropical rainforest and arid desert to windswept plains and freezing ice fields.

The world in a country

The country has mountains that dwarf Switzerland's Alps, vast, farming grasslands that rival the Midwest of the USA, desert landscapes as dramatic as Australia's, and a scenic Lake District ten times the size of England's. Whichever way you look at it, the landscape in Argentina is extraordinary. Even within one region there are great variations. So that, in the northwest, for example, the high desert of the Puna lies alongside

Penguins on the Patagonian coast

The northern desert

cows (and landowners), though soya beans are increasingly replacing cattle. In southern Patagonia, it is a very different story. Here, the relentless, windswept *steppe* (an arid area of scrub and grassland) gives little relief to any living thing. The stony soil supports only the hardiest shrubs, which sustain only the hardiest animals; the occasional volcanic eruption can cover huge areas with ash, and even Patagonia's sturdy sheep frequently starve in the worst winters.

Watery forms

With Chile as a bulwark against the Pacific Ocean, Argentina has only Atlantic coastline, but at 5,000km (3,107 miles) there is a lot of it. Over the millennia, the seas have pounded away at the rock, sculpting the dramatic arches and stacks of Monte León in the south. Further north are the rocky cliffs and pebble beaches of Puerto Madryn, and close to Buenos Aires are wide white sand beaches, though few people come here just to lie on the sand.

In lieu of a west coast, Argentina has its lakes – giant pools created by the Andes, when they broke through the surface of the earth and soared skyward. Imposing glaciers, tourist attractions in their own right, melt to form roaring rivers that water the lowlands. On the border with Uruguay, the estuary of the Río de la Plata is the widest in the world, and the Río Paraná that feeds it is second in size only (in South America) to the Amazon.

tropical jungle, where snaking rivers cut deep, red canyons, surrounded by snow-capped mountains.

Mountain high

Cerro Aconcagua (6,962m/22,841ft) is the highest mountain in the western hemisphere, the crown of Argentina's Andes, which form a string of toothy, snow-peaked mountains from north to south. Apart from this, the country is mostly flat, though the Sierra de Córdoba, in the centre, is a highland area whose highest peak is Cerro Champaquí (2,790m/9,154ft).

The fat of the land

This is a big country, but with a third of the population concentrated in the capital, much of the land is empty, with the largest horizons you are ever likely to see. The nutrient-rich 'black' soil of the flat pampas produces fat, healthy

History

10,000 BC Settlers reach the Andean and coastal regions of present-day Argentina, millennia after the first crossings of the Bering Strait.

4000 BC In the far south, the Yámana people build canoes and make it as far as Tierra del Fuego.

500 BC–AD 600 In the north, Tafi culture flourishes in Tucuman; they grow potatoes, broad beans and other vegetables. Ceramic cultures emerge in Jujuy, San Juan and in Catamarca, where the Condorhuasi herd llamas and live in round stone huts with grass roofs.

600–1480 Tribes master metal and bronze work techniques. Around AD 850, fortified settlements start to appear.

1480 Having completed construction of Machu Picchu, the Inca emperor Pachacútec heads south, conquers present-day northwest Argentina and integrates it into the Inca region called Kollasuyo.

1516 Spaniard Juan Díaz de Solis discovers Río de la Plata and claims it for Spain. Eaten by the Indians or killed by mutineers; either way it was his last voyage.

1536 Pedro de Mendoza creates a settlement on the site of Buenos Aires. Within five years, the pioneers are wiped out by disease and Indian attacks.

1580 The conquistadors try again, and this time stay put in Buenos Aires. All orders come from the Viceroy of Lima, the Crown's representative charged with looking after the southern territories.

1594 By decree of the Spanish king, all goods (mostly gold and silver) are sent overland to Lima, by boat to Panama, across the isthmus by land, and then onto ships for Spain; Buenos Aires is cut off.

1806–07 The British twice attack Buenos Aires, and the royal Viceroy tries to flee, but a militia of hardy smugglers, cattlemen and *gauchos* (cowboys) fight off the invaders.

1810   Buenos Aires sets up its own government – little more than a city council, but nevertheless a massive blow to Spain and the absolute power of the King – and seeks the help of José de San Martín in liberating the country from Spanish rule.

1816   On 9 July, Argentina's Congress formally declares independence, breaking with Spain forever.

1826–27   Bernardo Rivadavia is elected Argentina's first president.

1829–52   Argentina is dominated by the *caudillo* (landowner), Manuel de Rosas, who becomes the country's first dictator.

1879   General Roca massacres the indigenous tribes of Patagonia and is elected president the following year.

1910   100 years after independence, Argentina is one of the richest nations in the world, attracting millions of immigrants from Italy, Spain, Ukraine, Germany and other nations.

1939–45   Argentina declares its neutrality at the beginning of World War II. After Pearl Harbour in 1941,

Independence hero, José de San Martín is honoured throughout Argentina

discomfort grows with this position, until a military coup makes non-involvement a certainty. One of the coup leaders is Juan Perón.

1945 Argentina declares war on Germany, just as the allies close in on victory.

1946 Perón wins the presidency, promising higher wages and social security. His wife, Evita (Eva), is in charge of labour relations.

1949 New laws make it illegal to show disrespect for the government. Perón's opponents are imprisoned and newspapers silenced. He founds a party in his own image: the *Peronistas* are born.

1951 Perón is re-elected president with 67 per cent of the vote. Evita dies of cancer the next year, and his popularity then wanes.

1955 A military coup sees Perón flee to Paraguay and then on to Spain.

1955–70 Argentina spends 25 years flip-flopping between civilian and military rule.

1973 Perón becomes president again, but not before right-wing paramilitaries ('The Triple A') open fire on a rally to welcome him back.

1974–76 Perón dies and his third wife, Isabel, takes over. Strikes, terrorism and hyper-inflation ensue.

1976–81 Another coup. Police and army torture, repression, forced disappearances and extra-judicial killings of up to 30,000 people follow. Argentina wins the football World Cup in Buenos Aires.

1982 The regime sends conscripts to invade Las Malvinas (The Falkland Islands, as they shall be called from here on). UK forces re-take the islands three months later after a dirty, bloody conflict.

1983 The military government collapses and radical reformer Raúl Alfonsín is elected president.

1986 Argentina wins its second World Cup in Mexico, with Diego Maradona at the helm.

1989 — Hyper-inflation and political turmoil brings Peronist Carlos Menem to power.

1990–99 — Free market policies lead to hardships, strikes and crisis after crisis.

1999 — Fernando de la Rúa wins the presidency, and inherits a mountainous national debt of $114 billion.

2001 — Argentina falls apart. The IMF threatens to take away the cheque book, and a run on the banks to rival the Wall Street Crash of 1929 ensues. The country has four presidents within a fortnight amid economic mayhem, violent riots and shootings.

2002 — The peso is devalued, bursting the 10-year bubble of dollar parity. Another year of protests greets the harsh realignment. The IMF and the World Bank turn away in despair.

2003 — After winning the first round, former president Menem pulls out of new elections. Néstor Kirchner, another Peronist, is then sworn in.

2004 — A warrant is issued for Menem's arrest on fraud charges.

2005 — Laws that protected the military from prosecution for human rights crimes are scrapped. The 'Summit of the Americas' in Buenos Aires sees Maradona, Chávez and Morales lead huge demonstrations against George W Bush.

2006 — Argentina repays its $9.5 billion debt to the IMF. In Spain, Isabel Perón is arrested under suspicion of colluding with right-wing death squads when she was in power.

2007 — Britain and Argentina, separately, commemorate the 25th anniversary of the Falklands conflict.

Eva Perón casts her vote from hospital

Politics

If ever a nation needed a Nelson Mandela figure, it is this one. Argentina's leaders seem devoid of morals, ability and ideas, yet display a startling aptitude for embezzlement, populism and self-preservation. Past incumbents are as likely to appear before a judge, as to disappear when the going gets tough.

The Peróns

Juan, a military officer and admirer of Mussolini, was head of Argentina's Labour Department during World War II. He encouraged workers to unionise, introduced paid holidays, and cut the working day to eight hours. Before long, he was fired and jailed – his bosses afraid of his popularity, and that of his lover, the radio actress Eva Duarte. As the war ended, Perón was swept from prison to power on a wave of euphoria that Eva had stirred in the unions. During the election campaign, the widow colonel married the actress,

Eva Perón's tombstone

and Eva – nicknamed 'Evita' – was given Juan's old job in labour relations.

They promised a lot and over the next five years, they delivered. Industry was nationalised and productivity increased, schools, clinics and orphanages were built in the poorest areas, and even workers' holiday camps were constructed. At the same time Perón held on to his first love – fascism. Opponents were crushed if they got out of hand, and propaganda was the only news. When the economy faltered in 1951, the Peróns responded with further repression. Evita's death from cancer in the following year was the beginning of the end.

The wilderness

After Perón was overthrown in 1955, Argentina spent 25 years leapfrogging between presidents and generals, none of whom could fix what was broken. Meanwhile, Perón was in exile in Spain, living next door to Ava Gardner, who kept him awake with her film-star parties. At home, his still-popular party was banned from elections. When the country fell into chaos with armed uprisings, killings and kidnappings, the army relented and Perón returned. He had been president for fewer than eight months when he died in July 1974, leaving his third wife, Isabel, in charge. Weak and ineffectual, she authorised the army to 'annihilate' left-wing opposition, and by 1976 the generals, happy to work without a puppet, got rid of her.

The dirty war and dirty politicians

Political torture, killings and, most horrifically, 'disappearances' prevailed for the next seven years. Of course, the generals couldn't fix the economy but the Falklands conflict seemed like a good diversion.

When it all fell apart in 1983, Raúl Alfonsín took over, presiding over five years of hyper-inflation, riots and looting. Then Carlos Menem, a dyed-in-the-wool Peronist, took the hot seat. His two big ideas were to make Argentinians rich by pegging the peso to the dollar, and to change the constitution so that he could stay in power longer, allowing corruption and vice to prosper at all levels of government and business. Menem can be credited for the 2001 crisis, when the economy fell apart yet again, though by that time he had been forced from office.

A cleaner act?

Facing charges of embezzlement, Menem plans to stand for president again. In the meantime, Néstor Kirchner is in charge. He has paid off Argentina's debt to the IMF, partly restored stability and committed Argentina to long-term human rights improvements. Will this be his lasting legacy, or will Argentina's curse strike again?

The mothers of 'the disappeared' campaign for information about their missing children

Culture

'*That the world was and will be rubbish I already know...*
In the year five hundred and six and in the year two
thousand too.
There always have been thieves, traitors and victims of
fraud,
happy and bitter people.'

Cambalache *(Second-hand Shop), 1935*

The fatalism expressed in Enrique Discépolo's tango song *Cambalache*, is common in this country and characteristic of its most authentic art form. Tango originated in La Boca, the capital's impoverished port area. Drawing breath in bordellos and dance halls during the 1800s, it was born from the union of African slave rhythms and the already popular *milonga* – similar to the polka. By the beginning of the 20th century the music and dance had been appropriated by the wealthy and successfully exported around the world, but it has always stayed rooted in society here. Political repression in the 1950s spawned such a rash of radical song writing that the tango was

An artist's depiction of tango dancing in the streets of Buenos Aires

temporarily banned. In the 21st century, Argentinians go to a performance for the music, not the dancing. The lyrics are a powerful expression of sensibility and, although the moves may be passionate, the words are invariably melancholic.

A two-pesos coin was issued in 1999 to commemorate Jorge Luis Borges

Eurocentric

French-style café society, anglophile aspirations, and a language that is influenced by Italian words and intonation: Argentine culture is decidedly European. Immigration from Italy and Germany, along with intensive British investment in the 19th century, has left an enduring cultural imprint, with 98 per cent of today's population claiming European descent. Most Argentinians will even tell you that their history began with the arrival of the Spanish and, with the exception of the tango, there is little of the indigenous and African influences that characterise Argentina's near neighbours.

Well-read

Argentinians read more than any other nation in South America and Jorge Luis Borges (1899–1986) dominates the literary scene. Borges is widely said to be one of the world's greatest 20th-century authors, although he never won the Nobel Prize – some say because, despite early socialist tendencies, he failed to condemn the military dictatorship. Borges is best known for his short stories; he also wrote poetry

and significant essays, but never a novel. His work showed a preoccupation with national, introspective themes, such as *The History of the Tango* and *The Argentine Writer and Tradition.* He found an echo within the nihilistic ranks of the nation's intellectuals, declaring: 'The earth we inhabit is an error, an incompetent parody. Mirrors and paternity are abominable because they multiply and affirm it.' Perhaps this explains why Argentina has one of the lowest birth rates in South America.

Positive outlets?

Argentina's people are deeply scarred by their political history, rightly exasperated that, despite rich resources, they can never seem to break free from the cycle of poverty. This is often expressed as *bronca* – angry, social frustration that finds little positive outlet. Instead, a profound anxiety exists, which finds its chief expression in the country's psychotherapy culture: one in three adults and thousands of children attend weekly counselling sessions.

Indigenous people

When Argentina's first inhabitants arrived more than 20,000 years ago they lived in harmony with the unforgiving land, adapting to the territory and forming tribes as individual as the country's landscapes. Over millennia, they developed sophisticated languages and powerful shamanic religions. Colonist and missionary intervention in the 16th century brought white man's diseases, which silently exterminated most of the local population. The Spanish stole the pampas from the aborigines, seized the free-roaming cattle and fenced the land. Many natives were forced to relinquish their tribes, and work in the newly formed farms. These men were the country's first gauchos, although few Argentinians recognise the Indian in their national idol.

Leading from the top

According to the *Encyclopedia Britannica,* General Julio Argentino 'led a brilliant military career that included directing the Conquest of the Desert'. In this military campaign, vast swathes of Patagonia were cleared of natives in 1879 and 'Remington Roca' was elected president the following year. His face and the conquest are still depicted on the 100-peso note and children are taught that he is a hero. Yet the campaign was nothing short of genocide; the Indians had no firearms at all, while Roca's men were armed with the Remington Company's newest rifle, imported from the USA. Today, in Argentina, indigenous people make up just one or two per cent of the population.

The survival of the Mapuche people is threatened

The spirit of the indigenous culture lives on in the gauchos

The law of the land

It was not until 1983 that indigenous peoples received legal status within Argentina. The law, however, recognises them as just one homogeneous group, refusing to see the huge variations in language and traditions between communities.

In 1994, the Argentine Government signed up to a whole raft of high-minded constitutional amendments, one of which committed the country to recognising indigenous land rights. In practice, the communities do not own their ancestral territories, nor are they ever likely to. The military dictatorship of 1976 to 1983 made blatant seizures of Mapuche land, and landowners and multinationals continue this tradition of forced evictions into the 21st century.

A sad business

In the north, multinationals have bought up huge swathes of land, replacing forests with sugar plantations and fields of genetically modified soya. The Myba Guaraní people have seen their forests logged and pulped and, with the disappearance of the plants, their natural 'pharmacy' has gone too, leading to increased infant mortality rates.

The story is not much better in the south, where Benetton has purchased 1 million ha (2$^{1}/_{2}$ million acres) of Patagonia, with plans to exploit its natural resources. The Mapuche people, who have never regarded the land as something to be possessed – 'Mapuche' simply means 'People of the Earth' – are being denied rights to fish and access to drinking water. In 2004, after a local Mapuche family was evicted by Benetton, the courts awarded the conglomerate permanent ownership, ignoring the spirit of 1994's constitutional amendments.

As their lands disappear, more and more natives are forced into urban areas to look for work, and they make up a large part of the population in the slums known as *villas miserias*.

Festivals and events

'Carnival is more observed in camp towns than in the bigger cities, where the custom of celebrating it is very much on the wane, and where the law forbids water-throwing and other such damp forms of amusement, which are winked at by the more lenient authorities in local towns.'

Argentina from a British Point of View, 1910

Many public holidays are remembrances of political events rather than actual celebrations. Argentinians are not nearly as hedonistic as Brazilians, and **Carnaval** is now practically non-existent, just a few low-key parades in some parts of the country. Perhaps the biggest celebrations you will ever see in Argentina revolve around football, and their timing cannot be predicted. Look

Don't miss the *Doma* (rodeo) festival near Córdoba

out for heightened passions if the Selección (national team) is playing and big parties if they win.

In Buenos Aires, the main festivals reflect the city's preoccupations – tango and literature. The 10-day **Buenos Aires Tango Festival** in late February and early March takes place in various venues throughout the capital, with free classes, concerts and, of course, displays of this 'national sport'. For three weeks in mid-April to May, things are cranked up for the enormous **Feria del Libro** (*www.el-libro.com.ar*), Buenos Aires' book fair, which celebrates literature with readings and discussions. The third big event on the capital's calendar is **ArteBA** (*www.arteba.com*), the rapidly growing contemporary art fair held over five days at the end of May.

Outside the capital, events are a little more flamboyant. During ten days in January, the **Festival Nacional de la Doma y el Folklore** (*www.festivaljesusmaria.com*) near Córdoba is a cowboy spectacle on the grandest scale. The entertainment, mixing thrilling rodeo rides with folk music and comedy, starts at dusk and doesn't stop until the sun comes up. In Mendoza, the end of the wine harvest is celebrated with the **Fiesta Nacional de La Vendimia** at the beginning of March, with wine and song.

Inti Raymi (the Festival of the Sun) on the night before the summer solstice, around 20 June, pays tribute

Princesses of the Vendimia, the annual wine festival in Mendoza

to the Inca Sun God. It is celebrated in the northwest of the country, where indigenous Quechua culture is stronger. In the first week of October, the **Fiesta Nacional de Cerveza** (Oktoberfest) in Villa General Belgrano commemorates the founding of the town, particularly its European roots, with beer-drinking an obligatory part of proceedings.

Public holidays

In addition to those listed on pages 153–4, there are numerous regional public holidays. Businesses close and inter-city transport tends to be full during such times. If a public holiday falls at a weekend, it is normally moved to the following Monday.

Highlights

PARAGUAY

San Salvador de Jujuy

Antofagasta

JUJUY

SALTA

Salta

FORMOSA

ASUNCIÓN

Foz do Iguazú

Pacific
Ocean

Tucumán

TUCUMÁN

CATAMARCA

Catamarca

Santiago del Estero

CHACO

Formosa

Iguazú Falls

Parque
Nacional Iguazú

MISIONES

Corrientes

SANTIAGO DEL ESTERO

CORRIENTES

BRAZIL

Porto Alegre

La Serena

LA RIOJA

SAN JUAN

Córdoba

SANTA FE

Santa Fe

Río Grande

San Juan

CÓRDOBA

Mendoza

San Luis

ENTRE RÍOS

URUGUAY

Valparaíso

MENDOZA

SAN LUIS

Rosario

BUENOS AIRES

SANTIAGO

San Rafael

MONTEVIDEO

Río de la Plata

CHILE

ARGENTINA

LA PAMPA

La Plata

BUENOS AIRES

Concepcion

Santa Rosa

PAMPAS

Mar del Plata

NEUQUÉN

Neuquén

Bahía Blanca

Parque
Nacional
Lanín

RÍO NEGRO

Parque Nacional
Nahuel Huapi

San Carlos

Golfo San Matías

Manso River
Adventure

Trelew

Península Valdés

Parque
Nacional
Los Alerces

Esquel

CHUBUT

Punta Tombo

Atlantic
Ocean

Comodoro Rivadavia

Golfo de
San Jorge

Parque Nacional
Perito Moreno

SANTA CRUZ

Deseado

PATAGONIA

Parque Nacional
Los Glaciares

El Calafate

Bahía Grande

Parque Nacional
Torres del Paine
(in Chile)

Río Gallegos

Port
Stanley

TIERRA DEL FUEGO

Falkland Islands
(Islas Malvinas)

Punta Arenas

Parc Nacional
Tierra del Fuego

Isla de los Estados

Ushuaia

Cape Horn

N

Page	
26	Buenos Aires
48	Central and Southern Patagonia
66	Tierra del Fuego
76	The Lake District
90	Mendoza and Wine Country
100	Córdoba and the Central Sierras
110	Salta and surrounds

① Capital delights Swing to the strains of Tango in San Telmo or scream for your team at La Bombonera, the heart of football in Buenos Aries.

② Estancias Jesuíticas Follow the old trail between Jesuit estancias that are now a World Heritage Site.

③ Iguazú Falls Hear and feel these thunderous waterfalls – one of the wonders of the world.

④ Península Valdés Marvel at sea lions, elephant seals and penguins close enough to touch.

⑤ The ends of the earth Visit Tierra del Fuego – the land of fire and ice in southernmost Patagonia.

⑥ Parque Nacional Torres del Paine Trek through an unspoilt landscape of lakes and mountains in neighbouring Chile.

⑦ The greatest lakes Sailing, rafting and diving in pristine waters, hiking through forest and, in the winter, skiing too.

⑧ Wine country Sample a variety of world-class wines from the vineyards around Mendoza.

⑨ Salta Experience the distinct culture and landscape of this wild desert state.

⑩ The pampas Relax or ride horses at an *estancia* (ranch) and sample the gaucho life.

Sea lions rule on Península Valdés

Suggested itineraries

A word of warning: don't try to see too much on one trip. Argentina is the size of Western Europe and distances are huge. Most internal flights take at least a few hours and, ridiculously, almost always involve transit via Buenos Aires. With delays of up to several hours considered a matter of routine, travelling between two internal destinations can easily take a whole day.

Long weekend

Even a long weekend is enough to take in Buenos Aires and the pampas – the vast flat land just an hour out of the city by bus or car. Spend 48 hours in the capital enjoying some of its hedonistic pursuits, before taking off to *el campo* (the countryside) for some fresh air and luxury. Cabin crew, experts at squeezing the most from limited free time, will often spend their stopover in a welcoming estancia, relaxing by the pool or horse riding.

One week

One week is enough time to add a two-day trip to Iguazú Falls, including a visit to the Brazilian side, flying in and out of Buenos Aires. Alternatively,

The thunderous falls of Iguazú

look the wildlife of Península Valdés in the eye – flying from the capital to Puerto Madryn. You could spend seven days shopping (in the capital and San Antonio de Areco), wine tasting (around Mendoza) or trekking in the Parque Nacional Torres del Paine.

Patagonia's inaccessibility is one of its key attractions. Avoid a whirlwind visit and the whistle-stop tours that are often promoted. Top of many lists is the much-hyped, but admittedly spectacular, Perito Moreno glacier. Another favourite is Ushuaia, the southernmost city in the world. Both have convenient airports for ease of access, but on their own do not represent the best that Patagonia has to offer.

Two weeks

Two weeks would allow time for trekking in Parque Nacional Tierra del Fuego, with a visit to the less commercialised Chilean side, and then a flight to Bariloche, for hiking or riding in the Lake District. Rather than follow the hordes to Perito Moreno, why not visit the Tronador glacier? The road is less travelled and takes longer, but you won't be surrounded by bus – or boatloads of tourists.

Longer visits

With three weeks, all Patagonia's highlights are within reach, including the wildlife-filled Península Valdés, and the legendary Ruta 40 road trip. Add another week to allow for hiking the

Take it slowly to savour the magic

lakes of Torres del Paine, across the border in Chile.

Salta is the home of gauchos, imaginative, flavoursome cuisine and dramatic desert landscapes. This northwestern region, with its colonial churches, simple *adobe* (mud) houses and distinctive local crafts and wine, is arguably the cradle of Argentina. A week here can be tacked on to any of the itineraries outlined above.

Alternatively, spend your last week driving from the city of Córdoba along a route that takes in the atmospheric surroundings of the Jesuit estancias and peaceful mountain countryside.

Buenos Aires

Buenos Aires is South America's most European city, with its grand Parisian boulevards and Spanish-style plazas. Enjoy it as the porteños *(those born in Buenos Aires or in the port of Valparaíso in Chile) do, lingering in your favourite* barrio *(neighbourhood), and drinking fine wine and strong coffee. Indulge in local rituals; feel the adrenaline of a football game at La Bombonera and fall into the rhythm of the tango.*

BA, as it is sometimes known, has deep literary traditions as well as an emerging contemporary scene. This is a city of endless *reciclaje* (recycling), from the *cartoneros* who pick up the city's cardboard debris at night, to the reclaimed brick warehouses along the docks of Puerto Madero. The capital has largely shaken off its recent economic woes, with foreign investors snapping up properties old and new.

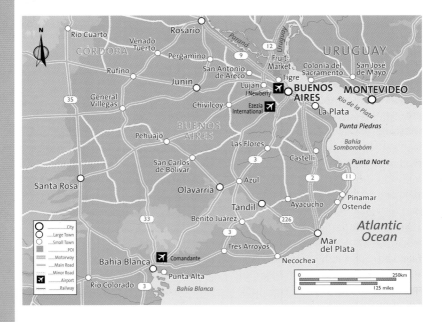

The widest street in the world: Avenida 9 de Julio

Within easy reach of the capital is cowboy country, where Argentinian gauchos still train wild horses in the pampas. Visitors can soak up some of the tradition on an estancia, tucking into enormous *asados* (barbecues) and riding horses. Don't miss lovely San Antonio de Areco, a centre for leather and silver craftsmen and the unofficial gaucho capital.

Mar del Plata is the seaside city where nearly the whole population of Buenos Aires decamps during summer. This and the World Heritage Site of the spectacular Iguazú Falls are both a plane ride away from the capital.

EL CENTRO AND PUERTO MADERO

El Centro (the Centre) is home to the capital's finest buildings, grand institutions and elegant historic cafés. Its main north–south artery, Avenida 9 de Julio, is wider than the Champs-Elysées in Paris. It is bisected by Avenida de Mayo, which has the Palacio del Congreso (House of Congress) at one end and the presidential Casa Rosada (Pink House) at the other. West of here, beyond Parque Colón, is Puerto Madero, a once run-down dock area that is being transformed into a cosmopolitan waterfront.

Plaza de Congreso

The centrepiece of the square is the Monumento de los Dos Congresos, a raised granite platform with a number of bronze statues by the Belgian artist Jules Lagae. On the highest plinth is a sculpture depicting the Republic trampling on the serpents of evil,

flanked by figures representing the 1813 Assembly and the Congress of 1816, when Argentina formally broke with Spain. The Palacio Congreso at the west end of the plaza is open erratically for guided tours of its opulent chambers. *Palacio Congreso, Entre Ríos and Callao. Tel: (011) 4370 7100. Phone for guided tour details.*

Plaza de Mayo

The Congreso may be the seat of Argentina's two-chamber parliament, but it is from the balcony of the Casa Rosada, which overlooks this square, that Juan Perón and Evita famously addressed the crowds, making grand proclamations in the days when their word was law. For most of the week the plaza is a tranquil lunchtime oasis, where office workers steal a kiss by the fountain, but on Thursday afternoons, mothers still protest the disappearance of their children during the years of dictatorship (*see pp4–5*). The building,

The grand façade of Casa Rosada

Dockside in Puerto Rodero

completed in 1885, is best seen at dusk when the ox-blood tint that was traditionally added to paint is not bleached by the sun. There is a museum of presidential memorabilia where guided tours in English can be arranged in advance, though they are often suspended for one reason or another. *Museo de la Casa Rosada, Av. Yrigoyen 219 (southern entrance).*
Tel: (011) 4344 3802. www.museo.gov.ar.
Open: Mon–Fri 10am–6pm, Sun 2–6pm.
Free admission.

Puerto Madero

This old dock area is being hyped by many as the city's next big thing, but at present it's not much more than a string of sterile (and generally overpriced) restaurants and hotels. However, a walk along the riverfront on a sunny day is quite pleasant – look out for fabulous old cranes that have been retained, old sailing ships docked on

the quay, and the striking modernist bridge that rotates to let ships pass. Things are more promising in the huge Reserva Ecológica Costanera Sur – perfect for a long stroll, mountain biking, or birdwatching (more than 200 species have been counted).

Teatro Colón

Undergoing careful restoration and due to reopen in May 2008, 100 years after its first performance, this theatre is the jewel in the crown of the city's cultural scene. Until then the fascinating behind-the-scenes tours have been suspended, but the show goes on – the opera, ballet and orchestral companies are on tour in locations around the city. The façade itself, overlooking 9 de Julio, is worth a look, before strolling past the gargantuan obelisk and stopping at Café Tortoni (*see p162*) for tea.
Libertad 621. Tel: (011) 4378 7344.
www.teatrocolon.org.ar

SAN TELMO AND LA BOCA

Try to visit the barrio of San Telmo, with its colonial buildings lining the cobbled streets, on a Sunday. Between 10am and 5pm, the streets are transformed into the Feria de San Pedro Telmo. It is more of an antiques market – in Plaza Dorrego and surrounding streets – than a fair, although impromptu tango performances do take place. The market has become something of a magnet for pickpockets, so keep valuables out of sight and try not to look too much like a tourist.

Treasures of San Telmo

At a price

Don't go expecting bargains, because there aren't any. Antique lace panels go for upwards of £100, century-old chandeliers are sold for over £1,000, and shipping home is extra. It may be that Argentinians, being a nostalgic lot, particularly value their antiques, or perhaps stallholders just see the tourists coming. The answer is not to have your heart set on a shopping frenzy.

In the neighbourhood

Visit instead for the lively atmosphere, slipping down a side street for a drink and a snack away from the main drags for a more authentic and low-key experience. Here you are more likely to be surrounded by locals than international tourists in search of a local steal.

La Boca

A stone's throw from the antique markets of San Telmo is the colourful barrio of La Boca, where every Sunday (and most days in between) the only subject worth discussing is football. On the tiny pedestrianised Caminito, brightly coloured houses hark back to the days when La Boca ('The Mouth' of the River Riachuelo) was the city's first port, and the impoverished locals would ask for leftover paint from visiting ships to liven up their homes. Today this street, with its cafés, artisans and tango dancers, attracts a fair number of tourists, but why come

Don't miss the thrill of the game

to Buenos Aires without visiting the spiritual home of Dieguito (little Diego)?

La Bombonera

Before Maradona was snapped up by Barcelona in 1982, he plied his trade with Boca Juniors here in 'the Biscuit Tin', a stadium whose steep, reverberant terraces and raucous fans have long intimidated opponents. Like the tango, which also began in La Boca, life in the Bombonera is a mixture of drama, love and heartbreak. When they lose, it's a tragedy, but when they win, and they often do, the neighbourhood goes wild. There are two football seasons here, but the more important, the Aperutura,

begins in August and climaxes in December. You can go with an organised tour, but seasoned football fans, who don't want to be herded around, should buy their tickets in advance from the ground, where it is much cheaper. Ask for a place in the all-seater *platea*.

Il Caminito

The most famous street in La Boca is, these days, something of a tourist trap. Tango dancers outside the cafés are looking for *propinas* (tips) in return for their photograph, and the craft shops are overpriced, but it is worth a look if only for the lively atmosphere and the distinctive painted houses.

PALERMO

Palermo is the oldest, largest and most popular barrio in Buenos Aires. The lakes and parks of Los Bosques de Palermo (Palermo Woods) and the boutiques, bars and restaurants of Palermo Soho and Palermo Hollywood – named after its TV and film production companies – are an attractive combination for both locals and tourists. At its heart is Plaza Julio Cortázar, more commonly known as Plaza Serrano. This is the start of Borges Street, where the famous author (*see p17*) spent his childhood.

Into the woods

Los Bosques de Palermo, also called Parque Tres de Febrero, was originally the decadent private playground of the dictator Juan Manuel de Rosas. It is possible to hire a boat on the artificial lake next to the formal but very attractive Rosedal (Rose Garden), while the small but perfectly formed Jardín Japonés (Japanese Garden) is worth a visit for its Japanese restaurant (*see p161*). The woods are criss-crossed by a number of busy roads but still the smell of eucalyptus often fills the air, with vendors on bicycles selling refreshments, making it a pleasant area to spend a couple of hours.

The planetarium, Planetario Galileo Galilei, is an obvious landmark in the 'woods'; the building, especially when lit up at night, is of much more interest than the rather poor shows about the stars in the southern hemisphere.

Two-wheeled tranquility in the Jardín Japonés

Sarmiento y Belsario Roldán.
Tel: (011) 4771 9393.
www.planetario.gov.ar. Admission charge.

Museums

MALBA (Museo de Arte de Latinoamericano de Buenos Aires)

This excellent and ultra-modern museum specialises in 20th-century Latin American art. Works by Mexican artist Frida Kahlo and Colombian Fernando Botero are on permanent display as part of a private collection of nearly 300 works belonging to businessman, Eduardo Costantini. *Figueroa Alcorta 3415.*
Tel: (011) 4808 6500. www.malba.org.ar.
Open: Thur–Mon noon–8pm, Wed noon–9pm. Admission charge.

Museo Evita

This polished museum in the house that the Eva Perón Foundation bought in 1948 does nothing to address the cult of personality that is responsible for her continued popularity in Argentina. Instead, it is a bizarre shrine to the woman, with various exhibits, including a video about the kidnapping

Boutique shopping in Palermo

of her body, as well as some of her old clothes. The courtyard café/restaurant is a definite highlight.
Lafinur 2988. Tel: (011) 4807 9433.
www.museoevita.org or
www.evitaperon.org.
Open: Tue–Sun and holidays 11am–7pm. Admission charge.

Shopping and eating

Palermo is the gastronomic and design centre of the city; wander around its streets and you'll find just about anything. Shops and restaurants change frequently, so pick up a free copy of the colourful booklet 'Palermo' at any of the local fashion shops or bars. The postcard-sized, up-to-date foldout leaflets have easy-to-read maps with descriptions and photographs on the following themes: *equipamiento* (furniture and art), *indumentaria* (clothes and accessories) and *gastronomía* (eating and drinking).

INSIDER INFORMATION: TALKING HEADS

Consult the government website (*www.bue.gov.ar*) for self-guided tours that acquaint you with the history of Buenos Aires through sound and music, including excerpts from political speeches and film transcripts. The 'voices of the city' can also be accessed on your mobile phone. There are 12 recordings covering 12 different areas of the city.

RETIRO AND RECOLETA

Heading north from Avenida de Mayo is the bustling shopping street of Florida, a narrow thoroughfare that feels claustrophobic, despite being pedestrianised. At its end, however, is peace and quiet in the shape of Plaza San Martín, the green oasis at the heart of Retiro. From this small district, the grand Avenida Alvear, lined with designer boutiques, leads west to where the city's great and not-so-good have found peace in the chaotic but ornate Cementerio de Recoleta.

Modern art in Plaza San Martín

Cementerio de Recoleta

For José Clemente Paz (see Círculo Militar, opposite), it was a short trip from the palatial residence of his final years to his eternal home here, in the city's finest necropolis. His tomb is one of the most ornate in this city of the dead, whose numbers also include Evita. Her final journey was rather more circuitous – her corpse travelled to Europe and was even kidnapped before she made it here. The immense cemetery is a mixture of grand designs, woeful follies, and rather sad, untended tombs. It is well worth an hour spent wandering. Around the necropolis, the market is a pickpocket's delight and the bars are overpriced.
Junín 1790. Tel: (011) 4804 7040. Open: daily 8am–6pm. Free English language tours Tue & Thur 11am (unless it's raining).

Florida's café society

Wonderful period architecture has been hidden behind sports and jewellery shops at the famous but dreary Galerías Pacifico shopping centre. Stick with Palermo for shopping and come to Florida only for afternoon tea and proper cocktails. The historic Confitería Richmond (*Florida 468. Tel: (011) 4322 1341*) is as elegant as the Tortoni, but with better service and without the tourist crowds. Closer to San Martín is Florida Garden (*Florida 899 esq. Paraguay*), an atmospheric bar and coffeehouse that was a popular haunt of intellectuals like Borges.

Plaza San Martín

When General San Martín's independence fighters where gearing up for battle, this is where they trained. Now it is one of the most peaceful places in the city. The grass slopes draw you up to San Martín's marble and bronze monument, where trees shield you from the noise of the city. Office workers take their shoes off and snooze on benches, while young couples take romantic strolls. Occasional exhibitions and performances surprise, but never intrude.

Around the plaza

The Edificio Kavanagh is one of the few buildings visible from the middle of the square. South America's first skyscraper, its art deco looks date from 1935 and were inspired by Manhattan's giants. On the southern flank of the square is the Palacio Paz, known officially as the **Círculo Militar**. It was built to be the largest residence in the country (it even has its own mini opera house) by a newspaper magnate in the *Citizen Kane* mould. Paz died before its completion in 1914, and his empire crumbled. Almost everything was imported from Europe and the building now houses a luxury retreat for retired military officers, though they deign to allow guided tours, usually in Spanish (*Tel: (011) 4311 1071. Mon–Fri 11am, 3pm & 4pm*). Walk north down the plaza's slope and you come to the understated **Malvinas Monument**, a small marble wall engraved with the 649 names of the country's sailors, soldiers and airmen (mostly young conscripts) who died in the Falklands War. Two sombre soldiers and an eternal flame guard their memory.

Grand designs in Cementerio de Recoleta

Maradona

Someone once said that footballers, like prostitutes, are in the business of ruining their bodies for the pleasure of strangers. No one fits the bill better than Diego Maradona, who was mercilessly kicked, elbowed and punched by defenders throughout his career. He endured years of pre-match painkilling injections; such was the value of even a half-fit Maradona on the pitch. During one hectic fortnight in the run-up to the 1986 World Cup, he flew four times between Italy and Argentina, playing two club games and two internationals and scoring four goals in the process; something which really took its toll.

Peak performance: Maradona in 1979

Reputations

When people talk about the best player ever, there is a shortlist of just two: Maradona and Pelé. People will always associate Maradona with controversy, amid allegations of Mafia association and drug use. Almost comically, he asserted that his first positive drug test, after a 1991 game in Naples, was a conspiracy – Italian revenge for defeating them in the World Cup.

The little onion in the biscuit tin

That drug test in Italy marked the beginning of the end – a career that began with Argentinos Juniors ('the Little Onions') and took him to

GOAL MACHINE

Maradona scored 345 goals in 678 games. England striker, Gary Lineker, scored three more than that, but Maradona was a midfielder whose main job was to create chances for others. This he did in abundance, though it is for the goals that dismissed Lineker's team from the 1986 World Cup that he will forever be remembered. One was FIFA's 'Goal of the Century', for which he single-handedly shimmied past half the England team (watching helpless in his own half, Lineker almost applauded) and the other was the 'Hand of God', scored minutes before, where he punched the ball past goalkeeper Peter Shilton.

Maradona still enjoys football to this day

Barcelona, where defender Goikoetxea, 'the Butcher of Bilbao' almost crippled him. Maradona won three Italian league championships, and along the way captained Argentina to World Cup victory in Mexico, scoring five goals and creating another five. His last games were played with his true love, Boca, and every Sunday he is back in the Bombonera (see p31), leaning precariously out of his family box, enthusiastically conducting chants and urging the team forward.

Alive and kicking

Understanding Diego is the key to understanding Argentina. In Villa Fiorito, the poor neighbourhood where Maradona first kicked a ball, people are desperate to survive and succeed – in life and in football. Tricking the referee is all part of the game and the 'hand ball' incident never hurt his reputation here. He has survived suspected involvement with the Mafia, pneumonia and a drug-induced heart attack, bouncing back to lead a mammoth march against George Bush in 2005. That same year, he hosted a hugely successful chat show, *La Noche del Diez* (Night of the No 10), trading stories with Pelé, and singing a self-penned football song to a tango rhythm. Pelé will always be 'the King', but in Argentina at least, Diego is God, the greatest player ever to wear the number 10 shirt.

BEACHES AROUND BUENOS AIRES

In the summer, all roads from Buenos Aires lead to the beach. Hordes head to Mar del Plata and Pinamar, while the élite scarper across the water to Punta del Este in Uruguay. The city is left to tourists and the service industry that surrounds them, while radio DJs and TV stars host massive beach parties for the holidaying porteños. Outside peak season and away from the crowds, beautiful forest-backed beaches within easy reach of the capital are waiting to be discovered.

Cariló

This tranquil resort 10km (6 miles) south of Pinamar is a great place to bring children. The forest beyond the sands lends itself to horse riding and mini nature treks, and the beaches are clean and uncrowded. For golf lovers, many of the hotels and apartments are within easy reach of the 18-hole golf course, which is surrounded by tall and majestic 80-year-old pines. For families looking for a few days of peace and quiet, BA Rent (*see p161*) can arrange lodgings in this area.

Sunrise at Pinamar

VILLAS MISERIAS

The 400-km (248-mile) stretch of road from Buenos Aires south to Mar del Plata is home to many poverty-stricken shanty towns. These have little of the gang rivalries that plague Rio de Janeiro's *favelas* (shanty towns), but in other respects they are remarkably similar. Immigrants from other provinces and countries live in these communities commuting to rich neighbourhoods to do menial jobs that others will not do. In return, the government provides almost no sanitation, roads, education, welfare or policing. What lighting and power there is must often be rigged up by the residents (an illegal act tolerated by the power companies who would rather not get their hands dirty). All in all, wealthy porteños do very well from the arrangement.

The busy beach of Mar del Plata

Mar del Plata

On the wide beach, tents, deckchairs and umbrellas are laid out in huge neat grids, with stalls selling beers, soft drinks and food never far away. With crowds of people milling around the narrow 'streets', it can feel like a chunk of Buenos Aires has been airlifted out and dropped onto the sands of Mar del Plata. For those in search of a bar-hopping beach holiday, it may appeal, though better options for this are probably available closer to home. Kids, too, might enjoy a short spell here. One option is the newly refurbished **Aquarium**, complete with water skiers, penguins, alligators and 3m-long sharks.
Martínez de Hoz 5600. Tel: (0223) 467 0700. www.mdpaquarium.com.ar. Open: Nov–Mar 10am–8.30pm and Apr–Oct 10am–6.30pm.

Pinamar

A five-hour drive from the city of Buenos Aires is the funky beach town of Pinamar. Among BA's beaches, this is one of the more chic, with the sands of Ostende a little to the south among the best dune-backed beaches anywhere in Argentina. A popular excursion involves 4×4 trucking though the forest, over the dunes and along the surfline, stopping off for a spot of sandboarding along the way.
Aventura Pinamar, Av. Linertador y Bunge. Tel: (02254) 493 531. www.aventurapinamar.com.ar

THE PAMPAS

Every flight attendant dreams of a stop-over in Buenos Aires, but the cosmopolitan centre is not, as you might suspect, the main attraction. The heart and soul of Argentina is little more than an hour away in the *estancias* (ranches), where gauchos spend their days in the saddle. Three hundred years ago, the residents of Buenos Aires were loath to leave their

INSIDER TIP: CHOOSE CAREFULLY

Some estancias are purely concerned with tourism but are, nonetheless, great places to spend a weekend. Others, even some of the most historic and prestigious of estancias, bus-in huge groups of tourists on whirlwind trips that make a mockery of the *día del campo* (day in the country). The experience is not recommended and no such places are included in this guide. The sign of a good estancia is if the owners are active in managing it, and will be there to treat you as their guest during your stay. If not, don't go.

city, believing the plains to be full of wild savages, intent on skinning them alive. In contrast, the gauchos, of mixed indigenous and Spanish decent, had been on the plains for a century, making a living from the hides of wild cows, and were prepared to defend themselves against attack.

Endless skies

On first sight, the countryside seems to epitomise the word 'plain' (the literal translation of *pampa* from the Quéchua language). For miles around, there is nothing but flat farmland, the monotony of which is only broken by the sight of the occasional cow. The magic of the pampas, though, is in the fresh air, clear blue skies, and 360° horizons that soon have visitors shaking off the city and reaching for the reins.

Riding the plains

Many working estancias have branched out into tourism to supplement their

Nothing but grasslands and empty skies

Saddling the horses on an estancia

income, or simply because the owners love the land and want others to share that feeling. A day-long ride on these ranches, with a knowledgeable gaucho leading the way, is an unforgettable experience – a world away from the dull lessons and uptight teachers that many associate with horse riding.

The finest estancias

Los Dos Hermanos (*see p163*) is a haven of rustic calm where you feel more like a member of the family than a paying guest. Juan, a splendid gaucho sporting a fine set of sideburns, will guide you through days of carefree horse riding, sharing his encyclopaedic knowledge of the countryside. The noisy donkey, Tito the buffalo and moonlight carriage rides will all light up your trip.

Patrice and his wife Macarena own and manage the heavenly **El Rocio** (*see p163*). Their love of the gaucho life, and Macarena's career with designer Hermes, are reflected in the immaculate villa, conceived by Patrice when he was just nine years old! Inside is furniture by the master craftsman Ricardo Passo, and the stables are full of priceless handmade livery from Patrice's favourite silversmiths and leather-workers.

These two estancias – for different budgets – offer outstanding value. Both have *sulkies* (two-wheeled carriages), so non-riders can take part too, and swimming pools where guests can relax. Each is special in its own way – if you can, visit both, and go on to find your own wonderful estancia.

Los Gauchos

'The Gaucho is invariably obliging, polite and hospitable. He is modest, both respecting himself and country, at the same time being a spirited, bold fellow.'
Charles Darwin, *Voyage of the Beagle*, 1836

From freedom fighter to farm worker

Because these nomadic cowboys lived alone and their indigenous forefathers had been wiped out, they came to be called gauchos, originating from an old word meaning 'orphan'. General San Martín was one of the first to honour them, when in 1800 he

Female gauchos hold their own in Argentina

praised their fight against the wild Indians. Before then, the free-spirited Argentinian cowboy had been branded lazy and rebellious. Yet it wasn't long before the wide expanses of his home, the pampas were fenced and, like the North American Indians, land taken from him. Today, the gaucho is a rare breed, likely to be working in an estancia as a *peón* (paid farm worker), although still displaying undeniable skill as a horse-whisperer.

Myth and man

The gaucho has always been a romantic figure, a mixture of earth and man, and so at one with his horse that he was said to 'walk without feet'. Literature has been largely responsible for this depiction. The epic two-part gaucho poem *Martín Fierro* by José Hernández (1872 and 1879) is a portrayal of a fictionalised everyman figure, while Ricardo Güiraldes freely admitted that his portrayal of the gaucho in his seminal novel *Don Segundo Sombra* (1925) was highly idealised.

A gentleman

Even today, the gaucho is upright both in posture and social standing,

The gaucho lifestyle is envied by many

contra punto – a singing match that often ended in violence.

Gaucho chic

Even today, Argentinians look to the gaucho, or at least the idea of the gaucho, as the ideal man – noble, earthy and independent. For generations, Eleodoro Marenco's decidedly nostalgic watercolours and black-and-white illustrations of gaucho life have graced Argentine walls, while Florencio Molina Campos' (1891–1959) entertaining caricatures continue to decorate calendars and place mats in homes around the country. Even youngsters, male and female, aspire to ride the plains with only their horse for company. Today, gaucho style is undeniably chic, with both fashion and interior designers cashing in on its desirability.

Tourism and the planting of crops such as soya may have taken over from the traditional gaucho way of life, but its essence is still very much alive in the hearts and minds of the Argentine people. Visitors can still catch glimpses of the real thing on estancias (*see p134*), in the gaucho capital of San Antonio de Areco (*see p44*), and at the Mataderos fair (*see pp123–4*). The highlight, though, is the annual Doma (*see p21*), where gauchos display their incredible horsemanship in a pulsating dusk-till-dawn rodeo.

wearing his stylish hat, distinctive *bombachas* (pleated trousers), and flamboyant yet functional *facón* (long knife), tucked into the back of his ornamental *faja* (belt). In days gone by, gauchos would swing their *boleadoras* (wood or stone balls) to catch wild horses and sing *payadas* (rural ballads). When it rained, they would sometimes visit the local *pulpería* (bar/local shop), drink *caña* (a kind of rum) and gamble on cockfights. There might also be a challenge to another gaucho of a

SAN ANTONIO DE ARECO

This lovely city little more than 100km (62 miles) from Buenos Aires feels more like a village, with its laid-back atmosphere, friendly residents and pretty river, once spanned by the country's first toll bridge (1857), which has been faithfully reconstructed using the original materials and techniques. This is the undisputed gaucho capital of Argentina and is steeped in history; bicycles outnumber cars here and the sound of horses' hooves echo through the cobbled streets. Incredibly, San Antonio, with its rich artisan traditions, pulperías and fascinating gaucho museum, has so far remained relatively untouched by tourism.

Gaucho capital

'On the outskirts of the town, about ten blocks from the central square, the Old Bridge spreads its arch on the river, uniting the country seat to the calm field.'

This description from Ricardo Güiraldes' novel, *Don Segundo Sombra* (1925), is still accurate today. Set in San Antonio, the book defined the gaucho (*see p42*) and the author is buried in a nearby cemetery. The Museo Gauchesco Ricardo Güiraldes, reached by a drawbridge in the Parque Criollo, is an 18th-century house containing authentic gaucho artefacts and paintings relating to Güiraldes. Attached to the museum is the 150-year-old Pulpería La Blanqueada, where wax figures play cards at the bar.

Güiraldes s/n. Tel: (02326) 455 990. Open: Wed–Mon 11am–5pm. Admission charge.

Artisans

The skills of San Antonio's artisans have been handed down from generation to generation. The absolute devotion to their craft and their final product are both extraordinary. It is a privilege to visit these silversmiths and leather-workers in the workshops (open usually by appointment) that showcase their creations. Pieces can be bought off the shelf, with commissions also undertaken. Prices reflect the time taken to make a piece – anything from a week for a decorative leather belt to two years for a set of intricately carved silver goblets or a set of unique gaucho reins.

Draghi: silversmith. (*Lavalle 387. Tel: (02326) 454 219 for appointment.*)

Gustavo Stagnaro: silversmith, with an impressive shop selling a range of crafts. (*Arellano y Matheu. Tel: (02326) 454 801. www.stagnaro.com.ar.*)

Raúl Horacio Draghi: leather, rawhide plaiter and silversmith. (*Guido 391. Tel: (02326) 455 499 for appointment.*)

Día de la Tradición (Day of Tradition)

This gaucho festival takes place over ten days in early November. The spectacular and authentic gaucho celebration is a special event with parading *tropillas* (groups of horses) and displays of horsemanship as well as dances and *asados* (barbecues).

Ruiz de Arellano Plaza

The town grew up around a chapel (1728) – now the Iglesia Parroquial (Parish Church) that dominates this elegant square. Don't miss La Esquina de Merti on the plaza (*Arellano 147. Tel: (02326) 456 705. www.equinademerti. com.ar*) a beautiful old pulpería that still functions as a bar and is a coffee shop and restaurant too.

Living history

Atmospheric tours by historic horse-drawn carriage (also by foot or bicycle) ride along the city streets, visiting the Gaucho Museum and the attached park, where creole horse and cattle herds are bred. Visitors are taken for a typical barbecue lunch at a family-run *parrilla* (grill) and tea at the local chocolate factory. Enthusiastic and knowledgeable guide Patricia Jacovella brings the area to life on such trips, introducing visitors to her artisan friends and having a drink with them in the local pulpería. Two-hour carriage trips from estancias take visitors along the Camino Real (Royal Road), through the city and into the countryside. Enquire too about the memorable moonlit picnics. Patricia also offers stimulating short immersion courses in Spanish.
Rivadavia 324. Tel: (02326) 453 674. www.livingyourspanish.com

Gauchos riding into town

Tour: Iguazú Falls and Parque Nacional Iguazú

The Iguazú waterfalls are the most spectacular natural attraction in the whole of South America. The huge horseshoe of waterfalls is 2.7km (1¾ miles) wide and 82m (269ft) high – nearly two and a half times the width, and 30m (98ft) higher than the better-known Niagara Falls.

This enormous curtain of water, formed by 275 separate *cataratas* (waterfalls), was named Iguazú (big water) by the Guaraní Indians long before Alvar Núñez Cabeza de Vaca 'discovered' the place in 1541. According to Guaraní legend, the waterfalls were created when an angry god split the river in two to prevent a young girl he was in love with from escaping by canoe.

Parque Nacional Iguazú

More than 2,000 sq km (772 sq miles) of subtropical rainforest surrounds the falls to make up this national park. Colourful butterflies and rainbows created by the spray from the

The spectacular Iguazú Falls

thundering water fill the air. Wild orchids can be seen; wildlife such as tapirs, giant anteaters and howler monkeys are harder to spot in the dense tropical vegetation. At the entrance are an interpretation centre, food outlets and the inevitable gift shops – some complain that the national park has become a commercial theme park. Mid-morning sees lots of tour groups, so try to avoid exploring the park at this time. For three nights every month, there are magical full moon tours. *www.iguazuargentina.com. Open: Oct–Mar 7.30am–6.30pm; Apr–Sept 8am–6pm. Admission charge.*

The best view is from the Brazilian side

See both sides
This UNESCO World Heritage Site is shared with Brazil and there is a certain amount of rivalry, with each country maintaining that its half is the best. The truth is that the Brazilian side has the better view because there are more waterfalls on the Argentine side, which in turn offers the most intimate, up-close experience. Most visitors choose to see the falls from both sides, spending a day on each, which is a good idea as bad weather can often mar the view. Although tour companies can arrange trips to Brazil – often reluctantly – a simple taxi ride will get you to the Brazilian side and back. Bring your passport and note that US and some other citizens require a visa to enter Brazil, which is one hour ahead of Argentina between November and February.

The train and the trails
From central station at the visitors centre, take the free Tren de la Selva (Jungle Train) that runs at regular intervals throughout the day. The first stop is the Cataracts Station, from where there is a path to the 650-m (2,133-ft) Circuito Superior (Upper Circuit) offering the best overall view of the Argentine side of the Falls as well as to the 1,700-m (5,577-ft) Circuito Inferior (Lower Circuit) with its close-ups of individual cascades and a not-to-be-missed free boat ride to Isla San Martín. The final stop is the Garganta del Diablo Station, from where a wheelchair-accessible *pasarela* (catwalk) leads to the edge of the 'Devil's Throat' – a spectacular sight that indeed roars with the force of the Falls. Additional walking routes include the 500-m (1,640-ft) Sendero Verde (Green Path) and the Sendero Macuco (Macuco Path), which takes walkers to the hidden waterfall of Salto Arrechea – a great place for a refreshing swim.

Central and Southern Patagonia

For hundreds of years, intrepid adventurers from around the world have made their way to the remote southern reaches of South America. In days gone by, it was the province of free-roaming indigenous peoples who wandered the plains, made camp beneath the Andean peaks and hunted the guanaco, a larger relative of the llama. Even today, Patagonia is a wild land, where settlements are separated by mammoth distances, and the people live a harsh, frugal life.

Hiking in the Fitz Roy range

Patagonia's Atlantic coastline stretches south from the pampas for over 3,000km (1,864 miles) to the very tip of the continent – next stop Antarctica. In some places, there are white, sandy beaches where visitors can swim, dive and engage in water sports. In other parts, it is a rocky, jagged frontier with the wild ocean, home to an astounding variety of sea life. Penguins gather in their thousands at Punta Tombo, where visitors can approach within touching distance. Huge colonies of sea lions and elephant seals can be seen on the pebble beaches of Península Valdés, and offshore, majestic whales leap into the air to provide whale-watchers with dramatic and long-lasting memories.

In the interior, the land is blasted by whistling winds so that plants grow low and wide, hugging the earth and supporting millions of sheep – one of the few large mammals that can live in this environment. Close to the sleepy town of Perito Moreno, ancient hands have crafted the Cueva de las Manos, a huge cave full of fascinating pre-historic art.

As the continent approaches its narrow southern tip, the Andes have created gigantic, dramatic glaciers and pristine lakes, accessible from the frontier town of El Calafate. Nearby is the hiker's mecca of El Chaltén – a gateway to the peaks of Cerro Torre and the Fitz Roy range. Across the border with Chile is Torres del Paine, a UNESCO Biosphere Reserve with imposing granite monsters and lush forests, dotted with mountain cabins where end-of-the-earth travellers gather to swap stories.

ATLANTIC PATAGONIA

Patagonia's northern Atlantic coast is a harsh, windswept environment, where penguins gather to breed, nest and shelter their young. In Punta Tombo, visitors can come within a metre of these fascinating, hardy creatures. Further north is Península Valdés, where spectacular sightings of southern right whales (*see p52*) draw thousands of tourists each year. Further south is the small fishing village of Camerones and, nearby, a reserve that shelters fur seals and guanacos. The first white settlers to this coastal region were Welsh, and the people are proud of their Celtic roots.

**INSIDER TIP:
NEW TRAVEL OPTIONS**

Until recently, those on a flying visit from Buenos Aires to Península Valdés had to fly in to Trelew, and then double back to Puerto Madryn. Now though, more sensible itineraries are possible – fly into Madryn and out again, skipping Trelew entirely, or drive south from Madryn, taking in all the coastal highpoints along the route, then fly onwards from the port city of Comodoro Rivadavia.

Puerto Madryn and Península Valdés

Visitors eager to encounter the bird and mammal life of Península Valdés start their tours in Puerto Madryn on the edge of the peninsula. It is a lively coastal

Child-friendly dinosaur in Trelew's MEF museum

A Magellanic penguin, Punta Tombo

city, with plenty of restaurants and bars catering to the thousands who come here to whale-watch between August and December. A highlight of any visit to the Atlantic coast, the peninsula can be explored as part of an organised tour (*see p52*), or ideally by car.

Trelew and Gaiman

The attractions of Trelew, one of Patagonia's main road and air transport hubs, are less obvious, but a real find is the Museo Paleontológico Edigio Feruglio (MEF), housing dinosaur skeletons and fossils from pre-history. For children, there is the chance to spend the night in the museum, exploring the exhibits with torches, learning about dinosaurs and sleeping among them. The nearby town of Gaiman is Welsh to the core, with grannies that still go to 'chapel' on Sunday and run teahouses for tourists. Nearby is the Bryn Gwyn field research station, attached to the MEF, which

offers tours to learn about fossils and Patagonian plants.
MEF, Avenida Fontana 140, Trelew. Tel: (02965) 432 100. www.mef.org.ar. Open: Sept–Mar 9am–8pm, Apr–Aug 10am–6pm. Admission charge.

Punta Tombo

When their chicks are strong enough, the penguin colony here begins its winter migration north to southern Brazil. While here, though, from September to April, these dinner-suited seabirds wander back and forth, oblivious to visitors who come close enough to hear their breathing. This is a once-in-a-lifetime chance to see the biggest penguin colony in South America, some years a million strong – the only rule is 'don't touch the birds'.

Camarones

Away from the crowds, further down the Atlantic coast, is this little village whose inhabitants work the land and sea. This is not an obvious tourist destination, but an annual fishing competition in February draws anglers from all over, and seafood delights in the shape of mussels, clams and octopus are on offer the whole year. The tranquil beach of Playa Elola is between the village and the Reserva Faunísta Cabo dos Bahías. Here, the endangered fur seal (closely related to the sea lion) has found protection from the hunters who value its pelt, Magellanic penguins feel at home, and guanacos wander the steppe.

Tour: Península Valdés

The southern right whale should really be extinct by now. Whalers thought it was the 'right' whale to hunt because it was a slow swimmer whose high blubber content made it float when killed. As it is, they continue to swim, eat and flirt off the coast of Valdés, albeit under the rapt eyes of researchers and tourists. A drive around the peninsula is a one- or two-day 400-km (249-mile) round trip, though those with less time can turn back after the whale tour and have lunch in Puerto Pirámides.

1 Istmo Carlos Ameghino

A one-hour drive from Puerto Madryn, the first stop is the visitor centre; pay the admission charge and learn about the wildlife you will encounter in the reserve. With more than 80,000 sheep on the peninsula, some farmers do not look kindly on the impact of the reserve on their business. Your visit and the income it generates can help to change attitudes.

From here on, the road is pebbles and dust. A further 25km (15¹/₂ miles) brings you to Puerto Pirámides. If you're

quick you may spot Maras (huge hare-like creatures) sprinting through the bush.

2 Puerto Pirámides

This village of 200 people was once a key supplier of salt to the beef industry, but now relies on tourism for its upkeep. If you're not in a rush, spend the night here. The nearby 'pyramids' are cliffs that really do resemble Egypt's Valley of the Kings.

Depart from Puerto Pirámides to see the whales that gather offshore.

Elephant seals make the ground shudder at Punta Norte

3 Whale-spotting boat trips

Although June to September is the best time for whale-watching, there are sightings right up until December. Your first sight of the southern right whale will probably be the V-shaped water spout from its unique twin blowholes. Only 4,000 of these wonderful creatures survive today, and in record years almost a third of those visit Valdés.

From Pirámides, head northeast to Punta Norte, 60km (37 miles) away, passing the sheep farms on your right.

4 Punta Norte

This is as far north as the endangered southern elephant seal has been known to venture, and is one of the few colonies anywhere that is growing. They come here to fight for a mate and breed (August to November), with dominant males having their way with a harem of 50 females in 70 days. Many pups return to moult (December to February), though some have been found up to 1,000km (621 miles) away in Las Malvinas (the Falkland Islands). Killer whales occasionally leap from the sea to catch the sea lions that come here, too.

Drive south for 35km (22 miles), past the pebble coves that surround Caleta Valdés on the peninsula's eastern shores. Look out for penguins, egrets, cormorants, terns and the feisty steamer duck, whose heavyweight credentials have scared off predators to the point where it no longer bothers to fly.

5 Punta Delgada

Surrounded by sandy beaches and overlooked by steep, imposing cliffs, this is another favourite spot for sea lions and elephant seals. The old lighthouse has been converted into a hotel.

Sea lion basking at Monte Léon

COASTAL SANTA CRUZ

Wool and petroleum are still staples of this province's economy, but tourism exploded when Kirchner was Governor of Santa Cruz. The downside of this is that only 5 per cent of Patagonia is protected in any way, and Kirchner took a *laissez-faire* approach to all sorts of developments. The coastal region lags behind El Calafate in terms of facilities for tourists, though in some respects this is no bad thing. Rich in history and biodiversity, the area has recently benefited from the Patagonia Land Trust's determined efforts to create a marine national park here (*www.patagonialandtrust.org*).

Laguna del Carbón

Much of the mainland here is below sea level, and is characterised by lakes, marshes and salt flats, but Laguna del Carbón, 18km (11 miles) from San Julián is special. At 105m (344¹/₂ft) below sea level, it is the lowest point in the western and southern hemispheres.

Parque Nacional Monte León

The importance of Argentina's coastline to the country's economy cannot be overestimated. Over-fishing in the last decade led to plummeting stocks and the loss of 20,000 jobs, to say nothing of the ecological cost. A first step to reverse this trend has been made in Monte León, where some 617sq km (238sq miles) of land and 40km (25 miles) of coastline have been converted into the country's first marine national park. The cliffs here have been mercilessly pounded by the sea, leaving dramatic rock arches and offshore stacks that attract thousands of birds such as cormorants and gulls. In the days when *guano* (bird droppings) was used as fertiliser, these islands were intensively harvested, and one of the wire lines that were used to haul the guano back to the mainland still remains.

On the mainland, visitors can expect to see herds of guanaco. Once there were millions of these in Patagonia, but the fencing of estancias for intensive sheep-farming decimated their numbers. Ironically, Monte León, where guanaco numbers are on the rise, is a former estancia. Around the shoreline, sea lions and penguins are attracted by the recovering fish stocks.

APN Office, Estancia Monte León.
Tel: (02962) 498 184.

Puerto San Julián

One of the few people to survive Ferdinand Magellan's pioneering circumnavigation of the globe was the explorer's chronicler. He regaled Europe with tales of *Patagones* – big-footed savages who were twice as tall as the explorers. In 1520 when the sailors came ashore here they did encounter the natives, and, although the Tehuelche people were rather tall, the rest was poetic licence. In the harbour, there is now a replica of Magellan's ship, *Nao Victoria*, complete with waxwork sailor figures. A simple cross commemorates the first mass to be held in South America, an evangelical affair where a number of Tehuelche were baptised. It would be another 300 years before the Europeans wiped them out completely.

Rigid hull inflatables take visitors on a breezy 90-minute tour of the bay to see the penguin and cormorant populations that live on Banco Cormorán and Banco Justicia. Wrap up warmly, and be on the lookout for dolphins. Another common sight is the anglers, who can be spotted on rocks, beaches and boats almost throughout the year.

Conservation efforts have seen a rise in guanaco numbers

Patagonian wildlife

Patagonia is renowned as a barren land where only sheep, shepherds and the occasional gaucho can survive. It is home to the world's fourth largest desert, larger than anything Australia or the US has to offer, and bigger even than Africa's Kalahari. Yet Patagonia's is also a coastal region, where the gentle slope of the land into the Atlantic forms one of the world's largest continental shelves – an essential habitat and breeding ground for a huge variety of marine life.

Ear to the ground

With biting winds whipping up vicious dust storms on the Patagonian steppe, it pays to keep a low profile.

Though difficult to spot, the land is alive with small, fast-moving creatures that specialise in scavenging. The tucotuco is a 30-cm (12-in) long rodent that pops its head out of its burrow only to look for food. The similarly sized cuis chico builds its own network of shallow trenches to move around in without being seen. The coypu is large enough not to worry too much about being seen. To the human eye, it is a scary beast, looking much like a giant brown rat – they can grow to more than 1m (3ft) long.

Mistaken identity

The mara or Patagonian cavy has, in many places, been forced out

Knee-high pudus hide in northern Patagonia's forests (see p83)

threatened; every year, off the coast of Patagonia, oil pollution kills 20,000 adults and 22,000 juveniles. These born performers put on quite a show at Punta Tombo, one of their major breeding grounds. Females lay two eggs, four days apart. In shifts, each parent goes foraging for food, while the other guards the young. Returning home, the forager waddles through the crowd of thousands, searching for his or her mate, before an emotional reunion complete with cries of joy by all members of the family.

Breach of a southern right whale

by sheep farming, but it is making a comeback in places such as Península Valdés. Looking like a cross between a rabbit and a deer, they have long hind legs, and grow close to 80cm (32in) in length. Often the mara is mistaken for the pudu, the world's smallest deer, and another Patagonian resident. Only 40cm (16in) tall, male pudus have antlers the size of a human hand.

The producers

The Magellanic penguin is something of a breeding machine, with almost four million of them around today – half in Argentina. Yet still they are

Star attractions

Undoubtedly, the penguins have top billing on shore, but when a 'beach master' elephant seal the size of a family car decides to fight a rival for his harem's affections, it can be quite a sideshow. In the ocean, the star is undoubtedly the 30-tonne southern right whale, the largest of the mammals seen in Patagonian waters, and the head of a cast that includes killer whales, baleens and minkes, as well as ten different species of dolphin, including the bottlenose and commerson, with its panda-like markings. Visitors flock to Península Valdés to see these giants, and sightings are common both from whale-watching boats and the shore.

RUTA 40 AND CUEVA DE LAS MANOS

Ruta 40 connects Bariloche in the Lake District with El Calafate in the extreme south of Patagonia, but it can sometimes feel like a never-ending road to nowhere. For many it is a big 4×4 adventure, as well as being popular with crazy motorcyclists who brave the gravel roads and biting winds that whip up the dust. Among the highlights are the rare sensation of absolute solitude in the great big Patagonian plains and the UNESCO World Heritage Site that is Cueva de las Manos. Here and there, you will meet gentle, easy-going Patagonians, but beware – peopled places are few and far between and that feeling of isolation may soon start to bite.

Cueva de las Manos Pintados (Cave of the Painted Hands)

Lying 160km (100 miles) south of Perito Moreno is the Cueva de las

Manos Pintados. The hike from the end of the road through the narrow Río Pinturas valley is atmospheric enough, but the cave itself is astonishing. The entrance to the cave, near the bottom of the valley wall, is three storeys high and 15m (49ft) wide. Inside, the painted walls depict hunting scenes, abstract forms and, mostly, the famous hands. Some have been stencilled around the *manos* (hands) of the artists and others

Don't expect traffic jams on Ruta 40

are positive imprints. The manos were stencilled as early as 5000 BC, but some of the hunting scenes pre-date even them by 2,000 years and are startling for their naturalism and diversity – some animals are ambushed, some are surrounded by groups and others are attacked with *bolas* (throwing weapons with weighted balls on the ends of interconnected cords).

Parques Nacionales (National Parks)

A half-day drive south of Bariloche, Parque Nacional los Alerces covers 2,630sq km (1,015sq miles). Its primary mission is to protect the country's largest forest of Patagonian cypress trees, some of which are 3,000 years old. There are good fishing and camping spots here. Parque Nacional Perito Moreno is about 260km (161 miles) southwest of the town that bears the same name, but the roads from Ruta 40 into the park are often in bad condition throughout the winter. The park is as isolated as you could want it to be, and is a fine place for those seeking some adventurous trekking. *www.parquesnacionales.gov.ar*

Perito Moreno and Los Antiguos

The unassuming little town of Perito Moreno is well placed for a visit to the cave paintings (below). Drop in to the Tintorería (*Mariano Moreno 955*) for some local colour. This old dye shop and laundry is now a ramshackle bar run by a charming octogenarian. Opposite, 'Mini Moo' has converted one room in her house into a small, private museum with photographs and relics of indigenous people collected during her lifetime. What's more, she can usually find you better lodgings than the prison-like hotel promoted by Chaltén (*see box*). Antiguos, 64km (40 miles) west of Perito Moreno, is a more obvious stopover choice, with comfortable lodgings on the shores of Lago Buenos Aires, and its own, more pleasant, microclimate.

Prehistoric hands made this cave art near Perito Moreno

THE FITZ ROY RANGE AND CERRO TORRE

The village of El Chaltén is just inside the border of Parque Nacional Los Glaciares, close to the Chilean border. Tourism here has exploded in recent years, and the isolation that hikers once felt here has somewhat dissipated; chances are, whatever trail you follow, you will run into fellow trekkers at some point. For climbers, Mount Fitz Roy and Cerro Torre have a special aura – although not enormously high, they are some of the most challenging climbs in the world.

Hiking and climbing in the Laguna del Torre

El Chaltén

In winter, this gateway village is deserted, recalling the late 1980s when it was hastily put together to prevent Chile from claiming the land around it. In summer, however, El Chaltén is packed with hikers and climbers, either full of eager anticipation, or exhausted, depending on whether they are coming or going.

Guided treks, climbing and cross country skiing

Within much of the northern zone of the national park there are hiking and trekking opportunities that are suitable for fit and able people without special experience. A guide is necessary, however, to find your way around safely, and there are plenty of agencies offering this service. Many offer beginners' courses in rock and ice climbing as well as more specialised training in long glacier traverses and ascents. The same companies generally offer Nordic skiing expeditions to mountain ranges around the park (*see p165*).

Hiking trails

Laguna de los Tres is a 25-km (15¹/₂-mile) trek offering some of the best views of Mt Fitz Roy (3,405m/ 11,171ft) and the narrow Poincenot needle (3,036m/9,960ft) to its side. At a push, the round-trip hike from El Chaltén can be done in fewer than nine hours, but many people opt to spend the night at the Poincenot base camp, close to the lake. From Río Blanco, the trail to the shimmering turquoise lake above is steep and badly eroded by the quantity of tourists, so care is needed over this last section, which will take about an hour.

Equally impressive is the one-day Laguna Torre trek, to the base of the four mountains that form the Cerro Torre range. From the lake, there appear to be four granite brothers in procession – Cerro Torre (3,128m/ 10,262ft) leads, with Egger and Standhardt in the middle. Bringing up the rear is the somewhat podgy Aguja Bifida. The shores of the lake are sometimes littered with chunks of ice that have come down from the mountains. Nearby, it is possible to spend the night at the DeAgostini base camp.

Neither of the above routes (which can be connected for a multi-day trek) requires a guide, but visitors should always be well prepared for changes in the weather.

Horse riding

El Relincho takes groups of five or six people up to the two scenic lakes mentioned above. The ride is not arduous and is suitable for beginners. The final ascent to Laguna de los Tres, however, must still be done on foot (*San Martín s/n. Tel: (02962) 493 007. www.elchalten.com/elrelincho*).

A burnt-out tree is a warning to avoid dangerous fires

EL CALAFATE AND GLACIAR PERITO MORENO

At the southern tip of the Argentinian mainland is the biggest single attraction in the whole of Patagonia. Named after the explorer who did so much to put this province on the map, the Perito Moreno glacier is one of the few worldwide that is not retreating, because more ice forms at the top than breaks away at the bottom. Another plus is that it is fairly accessible, yet in pristine condition. The town of El Calafate exists now pretty much for the sole purpose of providing food and lodgings for visitors to this and other glaciers in the national park.

El Calafate

Thanks mainly to Kirchner's hell-for-leather expansionism, this once sleepy

The advancing Perito Moreno glacier

INSIDER TIP: EXCURSIONS TO THE GLACIER

The National Park allows only one company to run each glacier activity. The many hotels and tour agencies in town differ only in the buses that take you up to the park, and offer little added value. For a more relaxed day, opt for a private car or taxi up to the glacier, and book your park excursion directly with the company in question.

outpost has mushroomed into a tourist playground, where development takes little notice of Calafate's privileged lakeside position. Brash new hotels spread out from the centre and more are under construction. Take special care in selecting lodgings – aim for something with character and that respects the environment, as listed in the Directory (*pp160–72*).

The Perito Moreno viewpoint

Every day, hundreds of visitors from El Calafate make the 80-km (50-mile) trip to the Perito Moreno glacier. The most basic tour for those on a whistle-stop visit is to the specially constructed glacier viewing platform. Before this was built, some tourists took their life in their hands by climbing down to the shoreline. The face of the glacier, 60m (197ft) high and 5km (3 miles) wide, advances relentlessly across the lake towards the viewpoint. Many times a day huge chunks break off and fall into the lake. Over months and years, the glacier pushes on but can then advance no further, and dams up the lake. Pressure builds, as do the crowds and

Trekking on the ice is a small taste of Antarctica

excitement on the viewpoint, anticipating the phenomenal rupture that will break the deadlock. There is a small café selling snacks, beer, wines and hot drinks, and visitors must stop on the way to the viewpoint to pay their entrance fee to the national park.

Glacier mini-trekking

Hielo y Aventura (*see Directory, p166*) employs 26 friendly and knowledgeable guides, who take visitors onto the glacier in groups no larger than 18, with two guides per group. To reach the glacier, visitors embark onto small ferries at Bajo de las Sombras for a 20-minute sailing to the south side of the glacier. Following a short introduction and safety briefing, and a 30-minute hike through the forest and shore, one hour is spent clambering around the icy slopes in crampons. The glacier quickly envelopes you, and before you know it you can see nothing but sky and the white and neon blue of the ice. Anyone aged from 10 to 65 can take part – the English-speaking guides will tailor the route to the ability of those in the group.

Other tours

There are plenty of variations on offer (*see Directory, p166*). Big Ice involves three hours on the ice, including a picnic. Estancia Cristina combines a half-day boat trip, sailing close to large floating icebergs, followed by a challenging horse ride through steeply sloping forest close to the glacier.

INTO CHILE: PARQUE NACIONAL TORRES DEL PAINE

A large number of visitors make the relatively short crossing into Chile to experience one of South America's most spectacular national parks. Covering more than 1,800 sq km (695 sq miles) between the Andes and the Patagonian steppe, this UNESCO Biosphere Reserve is named after the granite towers that reach up to 2,000m (6,562ft). Although these near vertical spires cannot be seen from within the park, it is the dazzling glaciers that sculpted them, along with sparkling turquoise and emerald lakes, which are the real attraction. Forests of *lengua* (native beech) trees, rushing waterfalls and snow-capped mountains provide a backdrop for magnificent sunsets and exotic wildlife, such as guanacos, pumas and condors.

A pristine lake formed by glacial meltwater

Getting there

The easiest point of access is Punta Arenas, 220km (137 miles) from Puerto Natales, which is 125km (78 miles) southeast of the national park. Lan Chile flies daily to Punto Arenas (four hours) from Santiago, with a stopover in Puerto Montt. Navimag (*www.navimag.com*) operates a four-day ferry service weekly from Puerto Montt to Puerto Natales and vice versa. If the weather is good, you may see icebergs and penguins and there is a guide on hand 24 hours a day. Try to book a cabin rather than a dorm, and don't expect a cruise. Alcohol is expensive (bring your own) and the food bland (go for the better vegetarian option and bring snacks and your favourite condiments).

Activities

Drivers (4×4 advisable) can traverse 100km (62 miles) of roads to many of the most popular sites via the three entrances operated by the national park – Laguna Armarga, Lago Sarmiento and Laguna Azul. A great way to explore the park is on horseback, but note that operators have to confine themselves to either the Chilean or Argentine side. Chile Nativo (*www.chilenativo.com*) offers trips from between 3 and 12 days. Big Foot (*www.indomitapatagonia.com*) organises ice walking and kayaking as well as climbing trips. Permits are required in this sensitive border region, so report to the national park office, or ask your travel agency.

Hikes

A network of trails throughout the park allows anything from one- to ten-day hikes. Try to come in the shoulder months of November/December or March/April to avoid the hiking hordes in January and February. The most popular hike is the 'W', which takes around four days, and the 'Circuit', for which you should allow up to a week.

Practicalities

A park entrance fee is payable and visitors must sign in. There are *refugios* (basic lodges with cooking facilities and bunk beds) that are pretty much all the same and it is usually possible to hire equipment for camping at associated sites. Book ahead whether staying in a hotel, *refugio*, or campground. Come with clothing for all conditions – the weather changes VERY quickly here. Also bring sleeping bags (not always available) and food, which is expensive in the national park. Although tens of thousands of people visit this area every year, it is not without its dangers. Always keep someone informed of your whereabouts and be careful around the often furious rivers.

Try to get hold of a 1:100,000 scale map for trekking: either *Mountaineering in Patagonia* by Alan Kearney or *Torres del Paine* by Daniel Bruhin. Visit *www.torresdelpaine.com*, an excellent site with photos, details of transport (with links), restaurants, hotels and maps, although since it is an advertising tool, its descriptions are rather enthusiastic.

Voracious grey foxes survive on hares imported from Europe

Tierra del Fuego

This archipelago was named by the first European explorers who, from their ships, saw the smoke from the Indians' fires. The mere mention of the 'Land of Fire' at the end of the earth ignites the imagination of travellers even today, although the jumping off point for the frozen lands of Antarctica should perhaps be called the 'Land of Ice'. Road links are improving, but most travellers still arrive here after a long plane ride, and those journeying on to Antarctica have another 1,000km (621 miles) of travel ahead of them.

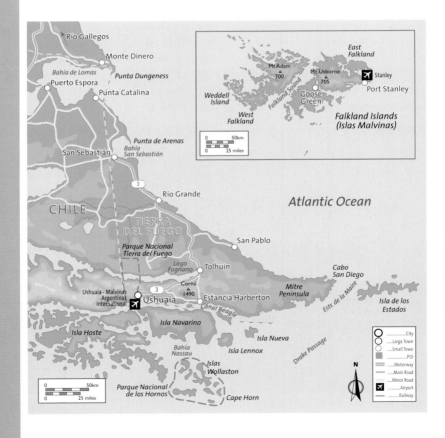

Even though the indigenous peoples had lived on Tierra del Fuego for 6,000 years, the Argentine government – in a political move to bolster its claims to Antarctica – established a penal colony here in 1902. In 1947, the prison was converted into a naval base, which now houses a museum that is one of the most visited attractions in the region. Argentina reluctantly shares Tierra del Fuego – an archipelago the size of Ireland – with Chile. The Falkland Islands are another source of friction (this time with the British) but in the last few years, they have taken on a new lease of life as a major cruise ship destination.

Ushuaia, the windswept capital surrounded by icy waters and snow-capped peaks, is full of souvenir shops and tourists eager to get their slice of the 'end of the world'. After visiting the city's museums illustrating the area's chilling history, most visitors use it as a base for exploring the forested national park, embarking on boat trips around the legendary Beagle Channel and even taking the trip of a lifetime to Antarctica.

The fiery sky above Ushuaia

Ferry crossings to Tierra del Fuego leave from Punta Arenas, Chile

USHUAIA

The tourist authorities make much of the fact that Ushuaia is the southernmost *city* in the world – the southernmost town is Puerto Williams in Chile. As a result, the once-ragged fishing village of wooden shacks now exhibits something of an urban sprawl, with a hotchpotch of Swiss chalets, concrete public housing and larger modern buildings. These all fade into insignificance against the huge backdrop of dense forest, scenic, snow-capped mountains and empty skies, where extraordinary sunsets regularly reduce visitors to tears.

Estancia Harberton

Missionary Thomas Bridges founded Tierra del Fuego's first estancia, 85km (53 miles) east of Ushuaia, in 1885, on land given to him by the Argentine government in reward for his work with the local Indians. Bridges' grandson, Lucas, wrote the fascinating *The Uttermost Part of the Earth* about the local Indians, and his son still gives guided tours of the farm buildings and English gardens. There is also a notable bone museum (*www.acatushun.com*) and a teashop.
Ruta J, Km 90. Tel: (02901) 422 742. Open: 15 Oct–15 Apr 10am–7pm. Admission charge.

Glaciar Martial

The modest glacier, within the national park, but easily accessible from Ushuaia, is best seen on a ten-minute, *aerosilla* (chairlift) ride (*open 10am–5pm daily, weather permitting*). Take a taxi or bus (summer only) to the lift, 7km (4 miles) northwest of Ushuaia, for sweeping views of the glacier, the city and the Beagle Channel. Serious hikers can walk along the

Camino al Glaciar (Glacier Road) from the centre of Ushuaia and at the end of the lift, climb up the mountain to the summit, which is 1km (½ mile) away. In winter, the glacier forms part of a centre for skiing; Cerro Castor, 26km (16 miles) from Ushuaia, is the area's largest ski resort (*www.cerrocastor.com*).

Museo del Fin del Mundo (Museum at the End of the World)

Housed in the historic stone-built Casa Fernández Valdés (1903), this small museum is decidedly eclectic. Four rooms contain stuffed birds, prisoners' personal effects, a recreated food shop and a figurehead of the *Duchess of Albany* – the English vessel that sank nearby in 1983.
Avenida Maipú 173. Tel: (02901) 421 863. www.tierradelfuego.org.ar/museo.

Ushuaia's harbour with the Andes beyond

Open: Nov–Apr Mon–Sun 9am–8pm, free guided tours at 11am, 2pm, 4pm & 6pm. May–Oct Mon–Sat noon–7pm, free guided tours at 2pm & 5pm. Admission charge.

Museo Marítimo y Presidio de Ushuaia (Maritime Museum and Prison of Ushuaia)

Despite its maritime moniker, the exhibits in the sprawling former *presidio* (prison) say more about the area's history as a penal colony. There are compelling life-size models of prisoners, many of whom were political convicts or serial killers. One interesting exhibit compares Ushuaia with world famous penitentiaries such as Alcatraz and Robben Island.
Yaganes y Gobernador Paz. Tel: (02901) 437 481. www.museomaritimo.com. Open: 2 May–15 Oct 10am–8pm. Admission charge.

Museo Mundo Yámana

Ironically, Yámana (the name of the first inhabitants of the region) means 'to be alive'. They, along with the Alakaluf, Selk'Nam and Haush indigenous peoples are now extinct due to European interference (*see p74*). This moving museum brings the Yámana culture to life with old photographs and maps.
Rivadavia 56. Tel: (02901) 422 874. www.tierradelfuego.org.ar/ mundoyamana (Spanish only). Open: Mon–Sun 10am–8pm. Admission charge.

Tour: Voyage at the end of the earth

Named after Captain Fitzroy's ship, HMS Beagle, the Canal Beagle (Beagle Channel) connects the Atlantic and Pacific oceans. Boat trips take passengers in the footsteps of Darwin, who traversed this steely stretch of water on the tiny boat of the same name. From Ushuaia, voyage times depend on the time of year and the destinations visited, and on whether you choose a traditional sailing boat or modern catamaran – the latter offers more comfort and is better in bad weather.

Canal Beagle (Beagle Channel)

Most half- or full-day boat trips pass the much-photographed Les Eclaireurs lighthouse, visit the sea lion colony on Isla de los Lobos (Wolf Island), the penguins of Isla Martillo and Bird Island's cormorants. Longer voyages go to Lapataia Bay in the national park or to Estancia Harberton. Some tours offer an opportunity to walk around the penguin colony or to visit Bridge Island, where the Yámana once lived.

Cruises

Book in advance for voyages of up to a week, leaving Ushuaia to Punta Arenas and Cabo de Hornos (Cape Horn) in Chile. These are cruises, usually with accommodation and meals on board, and prices reflect this. Ships sail

Close-ups of cormorants and sea lions on the Beagle Channel cruise

DARWIN AND THE BEAGLE

In 1829, a naval captain named Fitzroy was trading with Yámana natives in Tierra del Fuego, when one of his whaleboats was stolen. As 'payment' he simply took possession of four locals, and exhibited them to the King upon his return to England. The Admiralty ordered the return of Jemmy Button (named because he was bought for a pearl button) and two other natives – the fourth had died of smallpox. So, in 1831 Fitzroy and HMS *Beagle* set sail again, and this time along came a seasick-prone, 22-year-old naturalist – Charles Darwin. It was the beginning of a five-year voyage that led to one of the most important books ever written – *The Origin of Species* (1859). Rumour has it that, 30 years later, an understandably radicalised Jemmy Button took part in a massacre of Christian missionaries.

A luxury cruise around the channel

through a dazzling landscape of fjords, glaciers and forests, where Magellanic penguins can be seen in summer. Some vessels go 'around the horn', the legendary 425-m (1,394-ft) high promontory, where hundreds of sailing ships have been lost.

Las Islas Malvinas (The Falkland Islands)

Jose Luis Borges memorably described the Falklands Islands War in 1982 as 'two bald men fighting over a comb'. Firmly on the political map, this remote group of islands 500km (311 miles) from the Argentine mainland is still relatively unknown to tourists. However, an increasing number of cruise ships visit in the warmer months between November and March, docking at Stanley, the capital (*more information*

at www.visitorfalklands.com). It's a two-day boat trip from Ushuaia, with many vessels pausing en route at South Georgia and Antarctica and making landings using zodiacs (small inflatable boats). During the summer, migrating birds and marine mammals, such as penguins, dolphins, elephant seals and sea lions can be seen, with the remote rural existence of the population, outnumbered by sheep 220 to one, another draw.

Explorers – Darwin and Moreno

Charles Darwin and Francisco 'Perito' Moreno were two of the foremost explorers of their age. Like the conquistadors they were treasure hunters in this land; but for them the crock of gold was knowledge. Both Darwin and Moreno travelled to Patagonia with a hunger to understand the mysteries of nature, and both had barely turned 20 when they set off on their first great adventures. They were lauded by their peers and by the public, but in other respects their lives were completely different.

Portrait of Darwin in 1882

In the beginning
Francisco Moreno was born in Buenos Aires in 1852 and from a very early age had been fascinated by the exploits of other explorers. At the age of 19 he was sent some interesting samples from Patagonia, which convinced him that the wild region – at that time completely alien to most white men – was the place to go.

Darwin, born in 1809, had already been to university in Edinburgh and Cambridge when he boarded HMS *Beagle* for the trip to the far-flung lands of Patagonia. From a scientific family, he already had his doubts about the biblical version of creation put forward in the book of Genesis. He returned, in 1836, with his doubts confirmed but, perhaps wary of an establishment backlash, did not publish his *The Origin of Species* until 1859.

The savages of Patagonia
Despite his open-mindedness when it came to evolution, Darwin was very much of his time in regard to native peoples. Of the residents of Tierra del Fuego, he noted: 'A European labours under great disadvantages when treating with savages like these, who

ground rich in native artefacts. His subsequent report was published in Paris and encouraged European scientists to begin studying the native races of America.

Name calling

Moreno earned his nickname of *Perito* (expert) for the work he did on border disputes between Chile and Argentina. The two countries agreed to the British Crown mediating in the wrangle and, such was the strength of Moreno's arguments, that large tracts of Patagonia, which would otherwise have been Chilean, are today part of Argentina. Visitors will see many places named after the man: a national park, a glacier, a town, a street… As for Darwin, he has the Beagle Channel.

Moreno died penniless; he was given government land in thanks for his work, but donated it back to form the country's first national park. Before he died in 1919, he wrote: *'There is no place for my ashes, not even a 20cm by 20cm box. Yet if my ashes were spread out they might stretch across all the land I acquired for my country.'* Fortunately, a small island in the middle of Lago Nahuel Huapi was found for his grave, while Darwin lies in Westminster Abbey, next to the kings and queens of England.

Statue of Moreno in Parque Nacional Los Glaciares

have not the least idea of the power of firearms… Nor is it easy to teach them our superiority except by striking a fatal blow.'

While native life was cheap for Darwin, Moreno remained a staunch defender of indigenous rights, despite once being captured by Cacique Shaihueque, chief of the Manzaneros Indians. Whereas Darwin focused on fossils, plants and animals, Moreno's interest was more anthropological. On one of his first expeditions to Patagonia, he uncovered a burial

The train station marks its 'end of the earth' credentials

PARQUE NACIONAL TIERRA DEL FUEGO

This coastal national park, 11km (7 miles) west of Ushuaia, is a scenic area of empty beaches, salmon-filled rivers, plunging waterfalls and glacial lakes. Mountain ranges divide the park (not all of which is open to the public) into deep valleys where ancient Patagonian forests of *lenga* (native beech) are draped in 'old man's beard' (a wispy lichen) and in spring, Magellan orchids show their brightly coloured forms. Most visitors choose to visit as part of an organised tour and explore the park on foot.

Tren del Fin del Mundo (Train at the End of the World)

The original 'train at the end of the world' (*www.trendelfindelmundo.com.ar*) transported prisoners to the forest to chop wood for building as well as heating the new prison. Now distinctly touristy, it leaves from the Fin del Mundo station, 8km (5 miles) west of Ushuaia, stopping at a viewpoint before arriving at El Parque Station in the national park. Travelling independently by bus, taxi or bike avoids the extended stops on the train trip and is more interesting. Even if you decide to take the train on the outward journey, return under your own steam.

That's life

The Yámana inhabited Lapataia (meaning 'woody bay' in their rich language) and lived off the local seafood. When the settlers arrived in

1880, there were 3,000 Yámana; in ten years there were just 1,000 and in 1910 fewer than 100. All that remains of their settlements today are *concheros* (circles of shells and eaten molluscs that were used as tools). Birdlife is rich in the park, the dense forest a haven for parakeets, black browed albatross – some as long as 2m (6 ½ft) – and steamer ducks. Dams constructed by beavers introduced from Canada in 1948 have caused flooding and considerable environmental damage; be wary of any companies offering trips to see them, particularly if they claim to be ecotours.

Reach remote areas of the park by boat

On the trail

One of the best ways to explore the park is by following one of the short trails from the main road of Ruta 3. The Laguna Negra (Black Lagoon) 400m (1,312ft) from the road is a striking lake, coloured black from peat. A viewpoint 500m (1,640ft) from Ruta 3 leads through lenga forests to Lapataia Bay and sweeping coastal views. An 800-m (2,625-ft) 'Island Trail' follows the shores of Río Lapataia.

Those seeking longer routes should enlist the services of a guide. A challenging, 5-km (3-mile) Pampa Alta trail explores dense forest before giving panoramic views of the Beagle Channel; the coastal path from Ensenada to Lapataia is 8km (5 miles), but fairly straightforward. Cerro Guanaco (970m/3,182ft), the last Andean peak, is a steep 8-km (5-mile) hike.

Not on two feet

In the summer months there are plenty of alternatives to trekking through the national park. Many tours combine walking with a boat trip along the Beagle Channel and a stop at Isla Redonda for lunch. Horses take riders through the variety of landscapes, from dense woodland to the open shores of the bay. Mountain bikes can be hired from Ushuaia to tackle the hills and valleys of the park on two wheels. Canoes, the traditional mode of transport of the Indians, take tourists along the calm waters of the park's lakes and rivers.

Tierra del Fuego

The Lake District

The well-travelled but scenic Seven Lakes Road connects the two towns of San Martín de los Andes and Bariloche. The former is a pretty resort that attracts wealthy Argentinos. It is busy throughout the summer (particularly at Christmas and New Year) but nothing compared to Bariloche's centre, where busloads of graduating high-school students gather for daytime adventure tours and all-night clubbing.

The towns here are not the main attraction. Get out into the spectacular countryside that is Andean Patagonia's Lake District, one of the best family destinations in Argentina. Dotted around are magical retreats where you can while away the days, ideal for those in need of space, fresh air and relaxation.

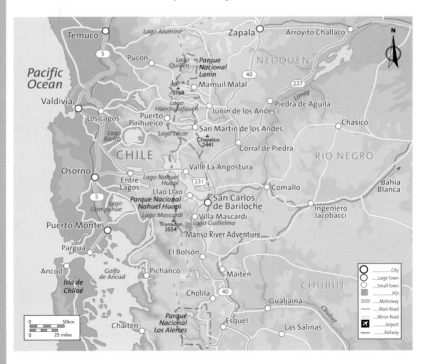

The area is home to three national parks, including Argentina's first, which was the brainchild of national hero, Perito Moreno. Summer days are pleasant, but not too hot, there are mountains and lakes, and innumerable activities for adults and children alike. This is a great place for rafting, kayaking, horse riding and other action pursuits. The trout fishing and birdwatching opportunities annually draw visitors from the US and Europe, as well as from Buenos Aires. Nature lovers will feel at home in the forests, hiking in an environment that is as safe as the countryside gets (no large predators, no poisonous snakes or spiders, and mild summer weather).

In winter, people come from all over Argentina to the slopes at Cerro Catedral, Bayo and Chapelco, and they are joined by more and more skiers from the northern hemisphere looking for 'summer snow'. Resort infrastructure is improving year by year, and the slopes, particularly Bayo, are drawing a younger crowd attracted by a fun après ski scene.

The Lake District

Head to the Lake District for an idyllic relaxing break

SAN CARLOS DE BARILOCHE

This small city, founded by immigrants from the European Alps, sits on the south shore of Lago Nahuel Huapi, whose waters are crystal clear and unpolluted. Aside from tourism, the only real industry here is the production of copious amounts of chocolate. Buildings are in the alpine style of stone and timber, cheese and chocolate fondues are a speciality, and waiters sometimes dress in lederhosen. For the best experience, look for lodgings outside the town.

Circuito Chico (Little Loop)

In town, they will tell you that this 65-km (40-mile) lakeside circuit can be done on bicycle, but many parts of the

A gaucho prepares an alfresco lunch

road are far too busy for any but experienced and confident cyclists. Instead, take a one-day tour, hire a car, or hop on and off the local buses, which will get you most of the way. Just outside town, at the Km 5 mark, you can take the funicular up to a revolving café on the top of Cerro Otto (1,405m/4,610ft). Or you can wait until Km 18, where there is a chairlift up Cerro Campanario (1,050m/3,445ft) with more panoramic views of the lakes and islands. The restaurant at the top is overpriced, but another 2km (1 1/4 miles) along the road is the turn-off for Península San Pedro. Detour here for a lakeside picnic, picking up supplies at Ahumadero Familia Weiss, a smokehouse specialising in hams and trout.

The famous Llao Llao Hotel at Km 25 is a popular but overpriced stop, and the views are as good elsewhere on the route. About 1km (1/2 mile) further on is Puerto Pañuelo, where tour boats leave for Isla Victoria (*see p169*). After Puerto Pañuelo, the road passes through a thick forest with well-marked hiking trails, before looping back on the southern shores of Lago Moreno towards Bariloche.

Horse riding tours

From Bariloche, a 20-minute drive east around Lago Nahuel Huapi takes you to Carol Jones' rustic shack, her base for horse riding into the hills and grasslands above the lakes. Twenty years in the business, Carol speaks good English and is helped by some amiable young gauchos. The rides are not action-packed, but are challenging in parts, and there is a real sense of isolation on the journey. Opt for a day-long ride with a meaty lunchtime *asado* (barbecue) in some shady spot, or take an overnight pack-tour deeper into the hills. All transfers from Bariloche are provided, and for pack-tours, all camping gear, but bring your own sleeping bag.

Cablagatas Carol Jones. Tel: (02944) 426 508. www.caroljones.com.ar

Museo de La Patagonia

With its range of stuffed animals from the region, this is a good place to introduce children to the wildlife they will see in the countryside. There are also interesting exhibits on the relics and lifestyle of the indigenous Mapuche people, who were practically exterminated by the Spanish.

Centro Civico. Tel: (02944) 422 309.
Open: Tue–Fri 10am–12.30pm &
2–7pm, Sat 10am–5pm.
www.bariloche.com.ar/museo

The spectacular setting of the Llao Llao Hotel

THE SOUTHERN LAKES

Bariloche itself is home to some big business tourism but, south of town, visitors can have a memorable experience in the rivers, lakes and mountains. A good starting point for all this is Al Sur (*www.alsurnh.com*), a select group of small lodges, restaurants and tour operators that exist in this area.

Cerro Tronador (Mount Thunder)

A one-hour drive from Hotel Tronador is Pampa Linda, where a forest trail leads to **Ventisquero Negro** (Black Glacier). The colour comes from the earthy mineral deposits that the glacier gathers on the way down Cerro Tronador. This peak, at 3,478m (11,411ft), is the highest in the Lake District and was named after the

Kayaking on Lago Gutiérrez

booming sound its eight glaciers make as huge chunks break away. Further on is **Garganta del Diablo** (Devil's Throat), a 335-m (1,099-ft) waterfall fed by the melting glacial waters. Organised one-day tours from Bariloche are available (*see p169*), but a night or two at Hotel Tronador is recommended, as there are plenty of hiking and horse-riding opportunities.

Estancia Peuma Hue and Lago Gutiérrez

Only 25km (15½ miles) south of Bariloche is this scenic idyll, where a few luxurious cabins, built with care and attention to the environment, are dotted around a mirror-like lake. The 360° views make your head spin, horses roam freely, the forest encircles you, and towering above are the jagged peaks of the breathtaking Cathedral Sur mountain range. Peuma Hue's caring owner, Evelyn, is eager to show you everything this extraordinary landscape has to offer: nature treks though the forest to hidden mountain lagoons, kayaking, windsurfing, rafting, trout fishing, horse riding and rock climbing. For a honeymoon retreat, there's a cosy mountain cabin, with a huge log fire and sun deck overlooking the lake. Aim to spend as long as possible here: it's a destination in itself, and most guests can't wait to return.
Cabecera Sur del Lago Gutiérrez, Km 25 Ruta 258. Tel: (02944) 15 501 030 / (011) 15 5101 1392.
www.peuma-hue.com

Lago Mascardi

The next lake south of Gutiérrez is the U-shaped Mascardi. A pleasant one-hour boat journey on the *Victoria II* takes visitors from Puerto Mascardi on the eastern shore to Hotel Tronador (*see pp168–9*) at the western extreme. The spectacular views and local organic food make this a good lunch stop. From the hotel, it is a 40-minute hike to a deep gorge and **Cascada Césares**, a series of three falls with a total drop of 70m (230ft).

Victoria II, Puerto Mascardi.
Tel: (02944) 441 062.
lmascardi@bariloche.com.ar

Río Manso

This river meanders around the southern Lake District before heading south and then west into Chile. Along its length there are some excellent spots for fly-fishing brook, brown and rainbow trout, particularly near Lago Hess. South of Lago Steffen, the river offers Class II and III rafting (suitable for children from 6 years old) and Class III and IV (for children over 14, previous experience recommended) as it roars westwards to the Chilean border. The routes pass through deep gorges and virgin forest, and can be combined with hiking and horse-riding expeditions.

The Lake District

Water the horses the natural way at Estancia Peuma Hue

PARQUE NACIONAL NAHUEL HUAPI

Argentina's first national park was inaugurated in 1934, thanks to Francisco Moreno (1852–1919), more commonly known as Perito Moreno (*see p72*). The man was a legendary Andean explorer whose goal was to 'preserve and demonstrate to future generations the richness of the Argentine Republic's natural flora and fauna'. In 1903 he donated close to 6,071ha (15,000 acres) of land around Lago Nahuel Huapi to be protected by the government. Today, the park covers 120 times that area and encompasses mountains, forest, several lakes and steppe – semi-arid grasslands where horses and cattle roam free.

Isla Victoria

Bigger than Manhattan Island, Isla Victoria, at the heart of the National Park, is a stopping-off point for boat tours of Lago Nahuel Huapi. The indigenous people gave Victoria its name, Nahuel Huapi (Tiger Island), but there are no big cats roaming the forest here. The tiger in question is the endangered *huillín* (southern river otter), whose only prey are crustaceans and fish. At points, the island is more than 4km (2½ miles) wide, but only 200m (656ft) across at its centre, with

Spend time on Isla Victoria to escape the whirlwind boat-trip crowds

INSIDER TIP: AVOID THE RUSH

Coachloads of tourists from Bariloche pile
onto a large catamaran for the 30-minute
crossing from Puerto Pañuelo to Isla Victoria,
but they spend, at most, three hours ashore
and many leave dissatisfied. A more rewarding
but pricey option is to stay at the island's only
lodge (see p168), where you can arrange
unrushed horse riding, fishing and nature
expeditions through the unspoilt island.

hilltops, forest and hidden lagoons in
both northern and southern parts. It is
easy to get lost in the forest, so guided
tours are essential. Birdlife is abundant,
though the otters, miniature deer and
wild boar are more difficult to spot.
Organised tours from Bariloche and Villa
La Angostura are available (see p89).

Península Quertrihué and Bosque de Arrayanes

In 1971, the rare Myrtle forest at the
southern tip of this peninsula was
declared a national park in its own right
– it was formerly part of Nahuel Huapi.
Wander through the trees and you can
understand why locals tell you Disney
was inspired by this place to create
Bambi – he did visit Argentina, but only
his assistants came to this part of the
country. The brilliant orange of the
trees, the vivid green grass and the
intense blue glimpses of sky are all quite
magical and continue to ignite the
imagination of visitors today. Short
visits to the forest are included in tourist
boat packages (see p169), but to avoid
the student tour groups in summer,
enter the park via Villa La Angostura.

Magical colours in Bosque de Arrayanes

Villa La Angostura

This small town at the northern tip of
Lago Nahuel Huapi is well placed for
exploration of the national park and its
largest lake, and the peaceful ambience
here is a world away from Bariloche's
hustle. Cross the small isthmus on the
edge of town and spend a whole or half-
day exploring Península Quertrihué on
foot, mountain bike or horseback. In
winter, the town is a popular but
expensive base for access to the ski
slopes of Cerro Bayo (see p89).

Tour: Manso River adventure

The Río Manso offers some of the most scenic and challenging rafting anywhere in the world, but also some of the safest, with experienced guides and reputable companies offering structured programmes with safety kayaks and overnight riverside camping. This tour is a three-day excursion along 55km (34 miles) of the best that the river has to offer, leading from the southern reaches of the Lake District to the Chilean border. Contact Extremo Sur (see p169) for departure dates and times.

Day 1

Depart Bariloche at 10am, and travel south along Ruta 258, past Lagos Mascardi and Guillelmo, arriving at Lago Steffen around 11.30am. Guides will provide a safety talk, before everyone changes and climbs into the raft. The tour sets off downstream, travelling 8km (5 miles) through Parque Nacional Nahuel Huapi's lush surroundings.

After this relatively easygoing run, the group cooks lunch on a beautiful sandy beach. From here on, the Manso

starts to get a little 'white'. Some of the rapids to be negotiated include Alka Seltzer, Billiard Edge, Hippopotamus Tooth, Switchback and Magnetic Rock; this is a Class II to Class III section.

Where the Río Villegas joins the river, it turns west and opens into the Lower Manso valley, with magnificent views of Cerro Ventisquero and Cerro Bastión. At the end of the day, camp is made beneath the stars at Piedra Pintada (Painted Rock). This is a chance to dry out those wet clothes,

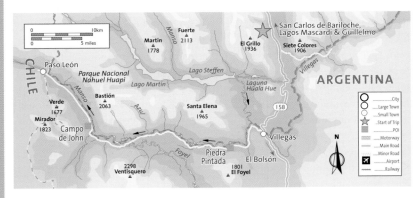

EQUIPMENT REQUIRED

Swimming trunks/costume
Sandals and trainers
Three T-shirts (synthetic fabric, not cotton)
  including one long-sleeved
Light shorts and trousers
Two fleece sweaters
Warm trousers (preferably fleece): advisable
  for camp wear (not jeans)
Rainproof trousers and jacket
Two pairs of socks
Sleeping bag
Towel and personal toiletries
Torch
Sunscreen and lip balm
Sunglasses (with secure headstrap)
Sunhat and warm, woollen hat

and go for a wander in the peaceful
forest before nightfall.

Day 2

After breakfast, it's back in the boats
for a section of the river that offers
amazing views and excellent fishing (if
your guide has remembered to bring
his fishing rod). Lunch offers a chance
to look back east at Cerro Santa Elena,

the mountain around which the river
has been winding its way so far. The
afternoon's rafting takes the group to
the confluence of the Río Foyel, and the
visual treat that is the hanging glacier
of Cerro Ventisquero, before going
ashore at Campo de John near the foot
of Cerro Bastión.

Day 3

Morning brings the last leg of the
Argentine section of the river. The run
is as beautiful as it is challenging, with
thick vegetation, alive with birds and
butterflies, overhanging the waterway.
Whitewater sections include the Velvet
Box, Ozone Hole, Shout and Turn,
Little Toboggan, closely followed
by Scrambled Egg (fear for your
breakfast) and finally, at the border,
International. The excursion finishes
at the Chilean Border, with a
lunchtime *asado* (barbecue) of fine
Argentine beef before the journey
by minibus back to Bariloche
(approx. 3 hours).

Tour: Manso River adventure

Challenging rapids on the Río Manso

PARQUE NACIONAL LANÍN

The northern part of the Lake District was designated a national park in 1937, and its scenery has, for decades, drawn wealthy visitors from Buenos Aires. Its prosperous hub, San Martín, gets busy in peak summer season and for skiing in July and August (*see p89*), but in general the area is less commercialised than Nahuel Huapi. Within the boundaries of the park are sprawling forests of native beech and *pehuén* (monkey puzzle trees); the hunch-backed, snow-capped Volcán Lanín (3,776m/12,388ft) dominates the western horizon, and there are countless lakeside beauty spots that are perfect for swimming, fishing and picnics.

Beaches

Just 4km (2½ miles) southwest of San Martín is Playa Catritre, where locals and tourists alike come to swim, windsurf and hang out in the beach café. Villa Quila Quina is a tranquil beach resort, backed by lush green forest on the south shore of the lake, and makes a pleasant day trip by boat from San Martín.

Boat trip on Lago Lácar

From San Martín's dock, regular tour boats depart on day trips the length of the lake, taking in Yuco, Isla Santa Teresita and Isla de los Patos (Duck Island). The boat passes the native Currhunica reservation and Villa Quila Quina before reaching La Angostura, where the waters of Lácar spill into Lago Nontué, generating a kaleidoscope of colours. Another 5km (3 miles) on, visitors disembark at Hua Hum Inn on the western end of the lake for a trek through the forest to Chachín waterfall. Lunch is provided at the Hua Hum Inn.

Hills and mountains around San Martín

From San Martín, which is at the end of a glacial valley, all trails lead up, and there are plenty of them. One-day treks include Cerro Huanquihue (2,285m/ 7,497ft), which takes around 14 hours, and Cerro Malo (1,945m/6,381ft), which can be done in less than

Cool down with a dip in Lago Lácar

Volcán Lanín rises above a monkey puzzle forest

10 hours, but is more challenging. Both begin with a hike up through the forest, which eventually thins out to reveal fantastic views of the lakes and forest below. For the more skilled and adventurous, a two-day ascent of the imposing Volcán Lanín involves a night spent at the refuge below the summit, before attempting the final climb to 3,376m (11,076ft).

Junín de los Andes

This town is a good base for those who want to do some serious climbing on Volcán Lanín. Interesting Mapuche handicrafts are on sale almost everywhere, and the surrounding area is known for its hunting (partridge, goose, boar and deer) and fishing (brook, brown and rainbow trout).

Ruta de Siete Lagos

Almost everywhere in the Lake District, you will hear about the Seven Lakes Road, the splendid scenic route that connects San Martín to Bariloche. There are countless coach tours, but in reality you will have more fun hopping from place to place at your own pace, either with a hire car, or by taking a *remis* (taxi) from place to place.

San Martín de los Andes

Development in this mountain resort has been wisely restricted over the years, so it still feels intimate, and even exclusive. There are good restaurants and hotels, and the location on the eastern shores of Lago Lácar is perfect for trout fishing expeditions, sailing and exploration of the national park.

Activities in the Lake District

With lakes, mountains, valleys and rivers galore, this is the place to come for adventure sports such as skiing, rafting and mountaineering, as well as more tranquil pursuits such as birdwatching and fishing. The choice can be mind-boggling, and you will be told at hotels and tour agencies that it pays to book in advance, due to high demand. However, it can be very dispiriting to watch the heavens open on the morning you have planned to go horse riding, so make reservations as late as you dare, ensure you can cancel, and have 'plan B' at the ready.

Kite surfing and wind surfing
Windsurfers take full advantage of Lago Nahuel Huapi's lack of shelter

True off-piste skiing in Cerro Bayo

from the wind and are, thus, a common site on the water. The water is, of course, pretty cold, and wetsuits are de rigueur. Kite surfing is slowly taking off here, too – beginners can easily get the hang of going in a straight line, but don't count on being able to change direction any time soon.

Paragliding
When the weather is right (good visibility and wind in the right direction, but not too strong) you will see people taking off from Cerro Otto and Cerro Catedral for flights over Lago Nahuel Huapi. It's safe for beginners flying in tandem with an experienced pilot, and does not require much effort beyond the initial run for take-off. For those who get the bug after their first time soaring silently through the skies (and many do) it's possible to learn how to fly solo with no more than five or six days of lessons.
Parapente Bariloche, Cerro Otto. Tel: (02944) 15 552 403.

River rafting and duckies
From San Martín, rafters can arrange expeditions down the Río Hua Hum or Aluminé (*www.tiempopatagonico.com*).

Pura Vida's kayaks can accommodate the mobility-impaired (*see below*)

For less involved expeditions, rafting near San Martín can be arranged by El Refugio (*www.elrefugioturismo.com.ar*). In the southern lakes, the Río Manso (*see p84*) is ideal for beginners and experts alike, and the scenery on the longer trips is truly spectacular. Choose between a six-person raft and an inflatable duckie – essentially, the same as a raft but for one or two people, and better fun for those with more experience.

Skiing and snowboarding

Winter sports in Argentina still offer good value for those seeking snow in July and August, and the resorts are continuing to improve. Cerro Chapelco (up to 1,920m/6,299ft) near San Martín is always popular with beginners and experts, offering 29 runs, the longest of which is 5.3km (3¼ miles). Further south, Cerro Bayo (up to 1,700m/5,577ft, *www.cerrobayoweb.com*) near Villa La Angostura is more youth-oriented, while Cerro Catedral near Bariloche is the choice of the Buenos Aires élite, but gets crowded in peak season.

Other activities

For horse riding around Lago Nahuel Huapi, contact Carol Jones (*see pp78–9*). A relaxed way to explore the lakes and rivers is by kayak and is an option often chosen by nature enthusiasts. Pura Vida Patagonia (*see p169*) offers good single and multi-day expeditions, has English-speaking guides, and can accommodate mobility-impaired passengers in their stable double-kayaks.

Mendoza and wine country

Lying in the foothill of the Andes, the city of Mendoza is in the region of Cuyo, which means 'desert country' in the Indian Huarpe language. The indigenous population built acequias *(canals) that remain today, irrigating the dry earth and giving life to the many trees. Mendocinos, as inhabitants of the Mendoza province are known, call their territory La Tierra de Sol y Buen Vino (The Land of Sun and Good Wine).*

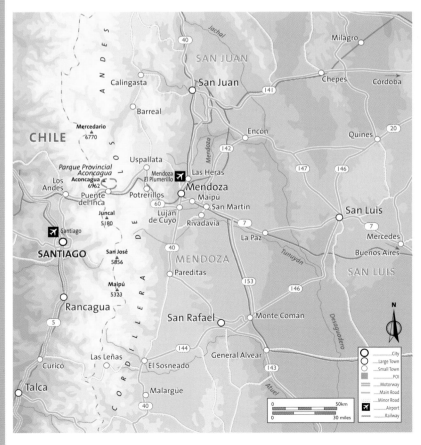

Bodegas

All around is wine country, which draws international visitors keen to try the area's wines. Each region has its own Ruta del Vino (Wine Route), where *bodegas* (wineries) can be visited for sampling and buying, and sometimes for dinner and overnight stays. For many people, a day visiting the wineries around Mendoza suffices; wine buffs and those who want to explore the countryside may choose to make a several-day tour, staying at bodegas on the way.

Gastro delights

Less well known outside Argentina is the area's reputation as a gastronomic enclave, where many of the country's top chefs have chosen to make their home. The province of Mendoza is the country's orchard, filled with perfect grapes, but also sun-ripened olives and plump peaches, and restaurant menus make use of locally grown produce to great effect. For many, the combination of fine wine and gourmet food is simply irresistible.

The countryside is a playground for adventure tourism – although many activities are distinctly seasonal. Skiing is big here between June and September (with a peak of July and August). Summer (November–April), when the snow melts and fills the rivers, is the best time for rafters. Walkers, too, will find the summer climate pleasant as they take to the hills, and even Argentina's very own Inca Trail.

Splash out on Mendoza's gourmet food and fine wines

Mendoza and wine country

MENDOZA CITY

The city known as the 'Garden of the Andes' is watered by the Río Mendoza and framed by low-lying desert hills and jagged snow-capped mountains. Mendoza is a world-renowned wine capital, but much more besides. The city's five plazas, lively nightlife that regularly spills out onto the streets, and friendly locals make it a popular spot to spend a few days.

City history

Museo del Área Fundacional (Museum of the Foundation Area) on the site of the old *cabildo* (town hall) traces the city's history from pre-Columbian times to present with artefacts and work by local artists.

Plaza Independencia in Mendoza

Videla Castillo between Beltrán and Alberdi. Tel: (0261) 425 6927. Open: Tue–Sat 8am–8pm, Sun 2–8pm. Admission charge.

Fiesta Nacional de la Vendimia

Every year the National Wine Harvest Festival celebrates the end of the wine harvest. During the first weekend of March the Queen of Vendimia is crowned, and festivities such as music and dancing and wine tasting take place in locations throughout the province. During this time, hotel reservations are essential.

Parks and plazas

At the heart of the city, Plaza Independencia is at the centre of four smaller squares: Chile, Italia, San

INSIDER INFORMATION: WHAT'S IN A BODEGA?

Most wine tours start in Mendoza and because the majority of bodegas have their own guides, who are often oenologists (wine-making experts) and usually multilingual, it is easy to travel the wine route independently. Wineries don't charge for tours or tastings, but it is essential to call ahead to make reservations and most close at weekends. The *Winemap* (*www.winemap.com.ar*, available in book and wine shops) is a collection of maps covering the main regions and, if driving, helpfully distinguishes between dirt, gravelled and paved roads. If you do want to go on an organised tour, the Grapevine (*Tel: (0261) 429 7522. www.thegrapevine-winetours.com*) has excellent, personalised tours by native English-speaking guides who are passionate about wine.

Martín and España. Take time to enjoy these mini oases; not so much for specific sights, but for their fountains, fairs and for being the focus of local, *mendecino* (Mendozan) life. Of particular interest is Plaza General San Martín with its pretty rose garden, and Plaza de Chacras de Coria, where an antique and crafts fair is held every Sunday.

On the edge of the city, Parque General San Martín is an enormous green expanse with a range of attractions. More fulfilling than the on-site zoo is the Museo de Ciencias Naturales y Antropologicas Juan Cornelio Moyano (Natural Sciences and Anthropological Museum Juan Cornelio Moyano).

Streets made for walking

Wide streets lined with poplars, elms and sycamores were made for walking; pavement cafés and restaurants make them perfect drinking and eating spots, too. Destroyed by an earthquake in 1861, the town was completely rebuilt on a convenient grid system. Avenue Sarmiento is a pedestrianised zone packed with shops, bars and cafés. Three blocks west of the main square, it intersects the ever-bustling main street of San Martín.

Mendoza and wine country

Bodegas store wine in wooden barrels to keep it at its best

Tour: A wine route

This route takes in the whole range of bodegas, from large, modern operations to traditional, 200-year-old wineries and family-run boutique bodegas. It covers the important vine-growing regions of Maipú and Luján de Cuyo, south of Mendoza, visiting six wineries, all of which require reservations by either phone or email. Websites are listed for all wineries; these usually feature history, maps and opening times, which are often unpredictable.

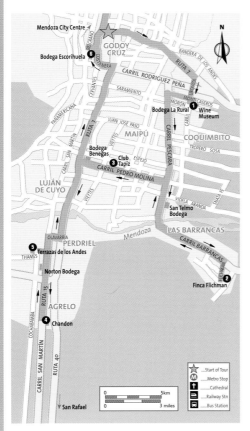

The 100-km (62-mile) circuit takes a leisurely two days but it can easily be shortened to visit just a couple of bodegas for those with little time or who would rather travel by bicycle. Otherwise hire a car – or preferably a car with a driver, making sure to agree a price beforehand. Drivers of either two- or four-wheel vehicles of course can't drink, and may be challenged by the poorly signposted, badly surfaced roads. The other option is to take a tour – either scheduled or customised.

Leave Mendoza on Ruta 7 in the direction of San Martín. Turn right onto Carril Urquiza and left to Montecaseros 2625.

1 Bodega La Rural

Just 12km (7¹/₂ miles) from Mendoza, this has been run by the same family for 200 years.

Its acclaimed Wine Museum with nearly 5,000 pieces is an excellent introduction to the area's viticulture, and makes this a perfect first stop. *Tel: (0261) 497 2013. www.bodegalarural.com.ar. Cross Carril Urquiza and turn left onto Carril Pescara. The canal of the same name runs parallel to the road and past San Telmo Bodega. Continue south aross the Río Mendoza where the road becomes Carril Barrancas. Turn right onto Flichman and continue to Munives 800.*

2 Finca Flichman

A hundred years ago the first vines were planted on a dried-out bed where the Río Mendoza once ran. Despite retaining ancient underground cellars from that time, this estate in Barrancas is one of the region's most modern bodegas. *Tel: (0261) 497 2039. www.flichman.com.ar. Return to Carril Pescara and turn left along Pedro Molina (no number) to Club Tapíz, 2km before the junction with Ruta 7.*

3 Club Tapíz

This highly recommended hotel is an excellent place to spend the night and awake refreshed for the next day of wine tasting. Reservations are essential. *Tel: (0261) 490 0202. www.fincaspatagonicas.com. Just after Bodega Benegas, turn left, crossing the Río Mendoza before turning right at Olavarría and then left onto*

Ruta 15, continuing south past Agrelo to Km 32.

4 Chandon

This slick operation, established in 1960, was Chandon's first operation outside France. *Tel: (0261) 490 9968. www.bodegaschandon.com.ar. Turn right onto Ruta 15, past Agrelo and Norton Bodega on the left, and then turn left onto Thames to Cochabamba.*

5 Terrazas de los Andes

This Spanish winery was founded in 1898. Today, grapes are grown at three different altitudes and there is a marvellous tasting room. Have lunch at the excellent dining room before taking a 3pm tour. *Tel: (0261) 488 0058. www.terrazasdelosandes.com. Return to Ruta 15. Turn right onto Olavarría and left onto Ruta 7. Continue all the way to the major junction with Costanera and turn left. Follow the road round and turn left onto Alvear and then left onto Belgrano 1188.*

6 Bodega Escorihuela

End the perfect day with a perfect evening meal at this bodega's sublime restaurant (1884 Francis Mallmann, *see p170*) before completing the last few kilometres back to Mendoza. *Tel: (0261) 424 2744/2698. www.escorihuela.com*

Fine Argentine wine

Argentina is the fifth largest wine producer in the world, surpassing every New World player except the United States. Most produce is, however, consumed domestically; not much makes it across the sea, so few of us have experience of it. Mendoza produces 80 per cent of the country's wine. The region's low winter temperatures and warm summers make for an ideal microclimate. Sand-clay soil and snow-melt irrigation provide perfect growing conditions, while the general absence of pests and mould ensures that the wines are essentially organic. The provinces of Salta and Río Negro, also at the base of the Andes, are increasingly being taken notice of as wine-producing areas.

THE ROOT OF IT ALL

Such was the Conquistadors' fondness for a drink that vine cuttings accompanied them to the 'new country'. When the local industry became too successful, King Philip II of Spain tried to ban production – a measure that had limited success right up until independence in 1816. By the end of the 19th century, Argentinian wines, centred in Mendoza, had really taken off. Increased European immigration brought an influx of vines with more modern techniques, and Argentina quickly became one of the world's biggest producers and consumers of wine.

A WINE TOP TEN – IN RED AND WHITE
Red

Bonarda The origins of this bold and fruity variety are largely unknown. Despite being the most planted grape in Argentina, Bonarda has so far been underestimated and is being watched with interest by experts.

Cabernet Sauvignon A full-bodied, tannic wine that often has overtones of blackcurrant and even chocolate. It is grown all along Argentina's wine route with great success.

Malbec Good bottles of Argentina's signature red surpass even those in France. Characterised by a full flavour with a certain earthiness, Malbec grows best in the Maipú region of Mendoza.

Merlot The warm plum and peppery flavours are often blended with Cabernet Sauvignon to soften its tartness. The grapes grow particularly well in the province of Río Negro.

Tempranillo This grape originally from Spain is grown widely in Argentina for its fruity, velvety qualities. Tempranillo is only now being used in high quality wines and being tipped as the next big thing.

White
Chardonnay The fruity, yet delicate, vine thrives in the Mendoza and Río Negro provinces. Like Pinot Noir, it is usually used as a basis for sparkling wines.

Pinot Noir This grape thrives in Mendoza's Valley of Uco, as well as in the Neuquén River in Patagonia and is most often used in sparkling wines.

Sauvignon Blanc Fresh, yet refined, this grape grows well in Mendoza province.

Torrontés The signature white grape is both floral and fruity and is produced to great acclaim in Cafayate, Salta.

Viognier The origins of this grape with flower and fruit flavours are unclear. Although little grown at present, the industry is hopeful about its potential.

Raising a glass
In the 1980s, successful and aggressive beer marketing made a

So many wines, so little time

huge dent in Argentina's domestic wine consumption. Wineries, forced to improve their product if they wanted a bigger slice of exports, began to attract foreign investment. Vastly enhanced technology, production methods and all-important marketing techniques have now transformed the industry. International wine critics have begun to sit up and take notice of the superb bottles being produced and in the 21st century the future looks bright for Argentine wines.

ADVENTURE MENDOZA

The countryside of the Mendoza region, framed by the Andes, is truly spectacular. Combine this with year-round warm weather and you have the ideal setting for all kinds of exciting activities. Its mountains appeal to climbers, and the snowy peaks are a playground for skiers. The lower hills invite hikers and horse riders and provide jump-off points for hang gliders, with the rivers whipping up white water for rafters. Look for tour companies that endeavour to take care of this fragile environment, as well as your personal safety.

Climb a peak

Cerro Aconcagua (6,962m/22,841ft) in the Parque Provincial of the same name is the highest mountain on the American continent. It is the ultimate challenge for climbers from around the world, but the summit is definitely not for the faint-hearted, nor those without a guide or extensive experience; acclimatisation and a minimum of three weeks is needed and many have died in the attempt. Much more manageable climbs are on offer in the valleys, gorges and cascades of Mount Penitentes and Vallecitos, both reached in three-day trips from Mendoza.

Take a hike

Half-day to week-long trekking trips tailored to different abilities are available year round. Many focus on the Aconcagua Park, with its river valleys and views of the great peak; from November to March is the best time to go. Road day trips take in the beginning of the historic pass into Chile – a natural gold-coloured stone formation known as the Puente del Inca (Inca's Bridge) – 175km (109 miles) from the city of Mendoza.

Hiking country in the shadow of Cerro Aconcagua

On the pack trail in Mendoza's wild countryside

Horse country

Take to the hills on the traditional mode of Argentine transport: the horse. Ride through pristine rivers, forests and mountains, you and your steed dwarfed by vast green spaces and majestic mountains. Trips last anything from a day to a month, with full-day tours leaving from just outside the city of Mendoza, and adventurous, longer excursions traversing the Andes to Chile, with an option to return by road. There are options for all abilities, although some companies have an age limit for minors.

Heavenly slopes

While less well known, and perhaps less attractive, than Cerro Catedral in the Lake District, the Mendoza region has the advantage of fewer crowds. Las Lenas (*www.laslenas.com*), 450km (280 miles) from the city of Mendoza, is the most sophisticated, and the

highest, offering a 1,200-m (3,937-ft) drop. Extreme and heli-skiers are in heaven here, but beginners and intermediates are well catered for, too. A large skiing area of 27 runs, high-quality snow and off-piste options are the main attractions. Los Penitentes (*www.penitentes.com*) and Vallecitos (*www.skivallecitos.com*) are the other main resorts.

White water

The fast flowing waters of the winding Río Mendoza provide for river trips ranging from straightforward, half-hour trips on Class II rapids to more exhilarating two-day tours on Class III to IV rapids. Potrerillos, 45km (28 miles) west of Mendoza, has become the area's white-water-rafting mecca. Although the season lasts all year, anyone wanting thrilling rides should aim to visit between December and April.

Córdoba and the Central Sierras

Many people say that if Buenos Aires is the country's heart, then Córdoba is its soul. It's a decidedly modern city but its two main attractions are the old-fashioned welcome of its inhabitants and the colonial-era Manzana Jesúitica (Jesuit Block). Argentina's second city, with its compact historic centre, is home to a large number of university students and graduates, but surprisingly few tourists.

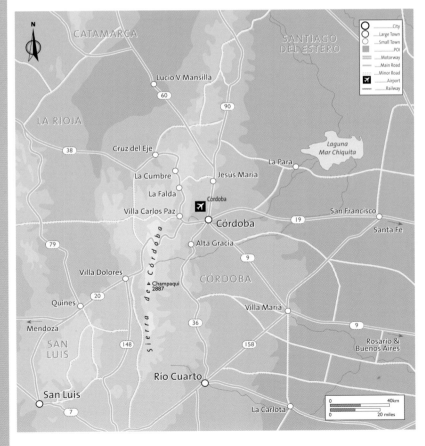

For years, the surrounding countryside of Las Sierras has been a summer playground for *porteños* (residents of Buenos Aires), and many houses in the mountains have their title deeds in the capital. As recently as 2000, the area's Jesuit estancias, along with the Manzana Jesúitica in Córdoba, were put firmly on the map when UNESCO named them as World Heritage Sites. They are linked by a little-travelled but scenic road – the Camino de las Estancias Jesuíticas.

A pleasant two- or three-day drive takes in all of the Jesuit estancias, through wild, rolling hills and past pristine waterfalls. Break the journey at one of the country's most luxurious estancias (*see p171*) or in one of the pretty hillside villages. At these charming settlements, sampling local produce and relaxing in the surrounding countryside is the order of the day. The energetic can take to hills on foot, bicycle and horseback, or even soar above in a paraglider.

The 16th-century Jesuit cathedral in Córdoba

CÓRDOBA CITY

Named after the city in Spain, Córdoba is also called La Docta (the Scholar) because it boasts the country's first university and today is home to no fewer then seven of them. Most visitors come to visit the Manzana Jesúitica, museums and churches by day and hit the good restaurants and lively bars of Nuevo Córdoba by night. Those who arrive from many other parts of the country are usually struck by the friendliness of the locals.

Argentina's oldest university

Manzana Jesuítica

Córdoba's star attraction is the site of one of the oldest universities in the whole of South America. Of interest within are the Jesuit church of Iglesia Compañía de Jesús (1671) with its baroque altarpiece, and the Capilla Doméstica (Domestic Chapel, 1644) (*guided visits only, 10am, 11am, 5pm, 6pm, admission charge*). The Colegio Máximo (Secondary School, 1610) and El Convictorio (Students' Residence) became the Universidad Nacional de Córdoba in 1622 (*open 9am–1pm and 4–8pm, admission charge*). The hushed cloisters and courtyards with their thick stone walls echo with more than 400 years of learning.

The surrounding Estancias Jesuíticas (*see pp106–7*) were set up in 1615 to sustain the Evangelist mission centred on the educational centre in Córdoba, but, in 1867, the Spanish king expelled all Jesuits from South America because

INSIDER INFO: JESUIT TOURS

Pick up the free leaflet *Camino de Las Estancias Jesuíticas* from the tourist office (in Spanish only), with details and floor plans of the city's Jesuit block and the outlying Jesuit estancias. Take a tour to best appreciate the city's sights, as information in English regarding the Manzana Jesuítica, and the other museums and churches is scant. The tourist office can provide details of themed tours – on foot, by bus or even by bicycle. Guided visits are given at set times throughout the day to major sites such as the Manzana Jesuítica and the Cathedral, and are usually available in English.

Córdoba's cathedral is still the centre of its religious life

they threatened his authority. Afterwards, the estancias were taken over by the Franciscans.

Jesuit missions

The Manzana Jesuítica, and the estancias that fed and financed it, are testament to the religious experiment carried out by the fiercely Roman Catholic Society of Jesus in the 17th and 18th centuries. They converted, and then controlled, indigenous peoples by fusing elements of Christian and indigenous values. Few guides or history books make even a passing reference to the Guaraní Indians whose culture was changed irrevocably for at least several hundred years, or to the thousands of African slaves who were used to build the Jesuit's small, but highly profitable, empire.

Plaza San Martín

Tree-lined, pedestrianised shopping streets radiate from this lovely, central plaza, which features at its centre the traditional statue of San Martín the liberator, seated astride his mount. The Iglesia Catedral dominates the western side of the square (*open 9am–noon & 5–8pm; admission charge for guided tours*). Work on the cathedral began in 1577 but took until 1784 to be completed – resulting in a predictably eclectic mix of styles.

Next door, the helpful tourist information office is housed in the white colonnaded cabildo, which was constructed in colonial style in 1785. It is easy to miss the Casa del Obispo Mercadillo on the northern side of the Plaza, but its fine wrought iron balcony is a colonial masterpiece.

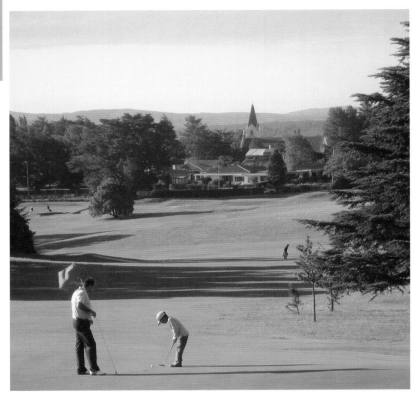

La Cumbre attracts golfers of all ages

VILLAGES AROUND CÓRDOBA

The region north of Córdoba is rich in lush vegetation, and the lovely hillside settlement of La Cumbre offers a relaxing atmosphere as well as active excursions against a backdrop of European scenery. The few and low-key sites are a welcome change from the high-profile tourism seen in other parts of Argentina. Do, however, avoid unattractive villages like Villa Carlos Paz – a magnet for holidaymakers who are bussed in from Buenos Aires.

HOUSE OF CHÉ

Guevara grew up to travel throughout Latin America, bringing him face to face with poverty and inspiring him to fight for economic equality for all in the region. Alta Gracia's small museum does not address the revolutionary's role in Cuba and Bolivia, where all kinds of Ché memorabilia sells in big quantities. Most Argentinians see him as a communist troublemaker and are disdainful of his role in history. Nonetheless, Jean-Paul Sartre described him as 'the most complete human being of our age' and he is undoubtedly one of the world's most famous icons.

Alta Gracia

This town on the western hills of the Sierra Chica, 35km (22 miles) southwest of Córdoba, grew up around an important Jesuit estancia (*see pp106–7*). Famously, the town was once the boyhood home of revolutionary, Ché Guevara – the **Museo Casa de Ernesto Ché Guevara** is his old house and contains personal effects, photographs and school reports. The young Ché was moved to Alta Gracia on the advice of doctors who prescribed its clean mountain air as a tonic for his chronic asthma. In 2006, Fidel Castro and Hugo Chávez, President of Venezuela, visited the museum, both paying homage to the communist guerrilla leader who, in 1967, was executed on Bolivian soil with the collusion of the CIA. (*Avelaneda 502. Tel: (03547) 428 579.*

Taking off over the sierras

Admission charge. Open: Mon–Sun 9am–7pm)

La Cumbre

Tranquil La Cumbre (The Summit), 1,000m (3,281ft) above sea level, was so named for being the highest point of the British railway built at the end of the 19th century. Many of the English engineers who were brought over to work on the project never went home. The mock-Tudor and rather snobby Golf Club (1924), distinctly British homes, frequent birdsong and the changeable climate give the town a decidedly English air. Many of the artistic local population have opened their studios as galleries and shops and established a number of European-style restaurants.

The town is world famous as a paragliding (known in Argentina as parapenting) centre. Even those who don't want to sit strapped to a chair with an instructor under a colourful parachute over the Río Pinto should visit the scenic lookout of Cuchicorral, site of the 1998 paragliding world championships. Weather conditions (especially wind) have to be right, so be prepared to wait for your flight.

Others choose to ride on horses, through a scenic landscape of streams and waterfalls, with condors flying overhead – either during the day or on a full moon tour with La Chacra (*Pasaje Beiró s/n. Tel: (03548) 451 703*). Hiking and cycling are also possible, though a guide is advisable.

ESTANCIAS JESUÍTICAS

In the 17th and 18th centuries, the Society of Jesus established educational, farming and cultural centres, using indigenous Indians and thousands of imported African slaves as labour. These self-sufficient communities were made up of cattle stations, fruit and vegetable gardens, fields of wheat and corn, *tajamars* (water reservoirs) with irrigation channels, windmills and carpentry workshops, as well as lavishly adorned churches.

Much is made of the economic success of this social experiment, which resulted in South America's first printing press and a unique style that fused local materials with European baroque. Yet little recognition is given to the local Indians, such as the Comechingones and Guaraní, who the Jesuits transformed from nomads to settlers and converted from sun worshippers to Christians.

Estancia Caroya (1615)

The exterior paintwork may be fading, but the internal courtyard has blooming fruit trees and the old cells house interesting exhibits relating to the building's history – including its role as a knife and sword factory during the wars of independence.
5km (3 miles) southwest of Jesús María. Tel: (03525) 462 300. Open: Mon–Fri 9am–6pm, Sat–Sun 9am–noon & 3–6pm. Admission charge.

Estancia Jesús María (1618)

On the edge of the town of the same name, this estancia was a successful bodega that still produces wine to this

In the middle of nowhere, Santa Catalina appears like a vision

The muscled Christ encourages hard work

bought by the mayor of Córdoba when the Jesuits were expelled, and is still owned by his family.

The highly decorated church, with its gold altar and carved balconies, is a wonderful example of baroque architecture. It was designed to impress the local population and convert them to Christianity. The Christ on a cross has articulated arms so that the Indians could see the deity in a human form and a porcelain, doll-like, Mary has real hair. The estancia included the Jesuits' main centre of cattle breeding, as well as workshops with looms and two mills. *La ranchería* (the slave quarters) is now a shop and bar.

20km (12 miles) northwest of Jesús María. Tel: (03525) 421 600. Open: Apr–Sept Tue–Sun 10am–1pm & 2–6pm, Oct–Mar Tue–Sun 10am–1pm & 3–7.30pm. Admission charge. Guided tours available.

day. A museum, Museo Jesuítico Nacional de Jesús María contains more than 10,000 artefacts from the indigenous people throughout Argentina and there is a simple church.
48km (30 miles) north of Córdoba. Tel: (03525) 420 126. Open: Mon–Fri 9am–6pm, Sat–Sun 10am–noon & 3–6pm. Admission charge.

Estancia Santa Catalina (1622)

The sight of this enormous, solitary, white church at the end of a dirt road is extraordinary – like seeing a cathedral appear in the middle of a field. It is the biggest and one of the best-preserved estancias, and is privately owned. It was

Estancia Alta Gracia (1643)

This, the most active of all of the Jesuit estancias, includes the Iglesia Parroquial Nuestra Señora de la Merced, which is still the local parish church. The Museo Histórico Nacional Casa del Virrey Liniers (the house of the viceroy for just a few months in 1810) is one of the few Jesuit estancias to acknowledge the local Indians.
Alta Gracia, main square. Tel: (03547) 421 303. www.museoliniers.org.ar. Open: Tue–Sun 9.30am–8pm summer, Tue–Sun 9.30am–12.30pm & 3.30–6.30pm winter. Admission charge.

Tour: A hillside drive

Take this lovely two-day, 300-km (186-mile) circuit from Córdoba through unspoilt countryside, where seemingly crumpled mountains rise out of the lush, tree-covered land. After walking around the Manzana Jesuítica in Córdoba, continue the theme, with visits to four Jesuit estancias (all clearly signposted) and hillside settlements. Most of the roads are excellent, with some sections on dirt tracks. Those who don't want to hire a car can take a very reasonably priced taxi (agree a figure before setting off), either in stages or for the whole drive. Sections between main settlements can also be completed by bus, with taxis to the estancias. From Córdoba, travel north along Ruta 9 for 43km (27 miles).

1 Estancia Caroya

The fascinating Estancia Caroya (*see p106*) is clearly signposted from the main road.

Return to Ruta 9 and continue for 5km (3 miles) to Jesús María.

2 Jesús María

The working town of Jesús María is home to the estancia of the same name (*see p106*) and the Festival Nacional de la Doma y el Folklore (National Rodeo and Folklore Festival) (*www.festivaljesusmaria.com Spanish only*). This gaucho rodeo delights visitors for 10 days (9am–5pm) in January and is probably Argentina's most important and authentic festival.

Leave Jesús María on the road leading west to Asochinga. After 11km (7 miles) turn right along a heavily forested dirt road heading northwest and continue for 19km (12 miles).

3 Estancia Santa Catalina

(*See p107*) This estancia is a marvellous sight, matched by its setting.

Travel 14km (9 miles) south to Asochinga by winding dirt road and then turn right to La Cumbre. The unpaved and often stony road on this section is perhaps the highlight of this drive. Follow the Camino Viejo (an old mule road) through beautiful, uninhabited rolling hills. There are no facilities on this section and very little traffic.

4 La Cumbre

Stop for a night or even two at the restful Hotel Victoria in La Cumbre (*see p171*), 96km (60 miles) from Córdoba.

Take Ruta 38 south through forested La Falda on the western slopes of the Sierra Chica nearly 1,000m (3,281ft) above sea level.

5 Estancia La Candelaria

From here it is a 50-km (31-mile) detour west to Estancia La Candelaria, built in 1683 as a fortified sanctuary. *Return along the same road to re-join Ruta 38 southwards until you reach Cosquín with its pretty bridge. Ceramic pots and painted pigs are laid out for* sale on many sections of the road, and the enormous reservoir of **San Roque** appears on the right near Villa Carlos Paz. Follow the signs back to Córdoba, but if you still have room for one last Jesuit estancia, make a 35-km (22-mile) detour southwest from Cordoba along Ruta 5 to Alta Gracia.

6 Alta Gracia

At the town of Alta Gracia is the Jesuit estancia of the same name (*see p107*).

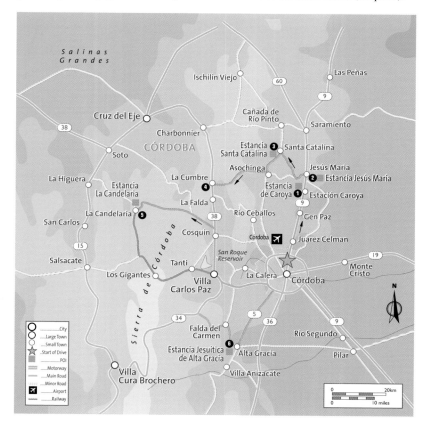

Salta and surrounds

There is some kind of magic in the air in this corner of northwest Argentina. The big, blue skies and immense desert vistas, dotted with herds of llama and vicuña, have changed little since the region formed the southernmost reaches of the Inca Empire. Salta means 'beautiful' in Quechua, and in the tiny mountain villages, where the land is crisscrossed with Inca trails, lifestyles do indeed stay true to time-honoured peasant traditions of strength, simplicity and beauty.

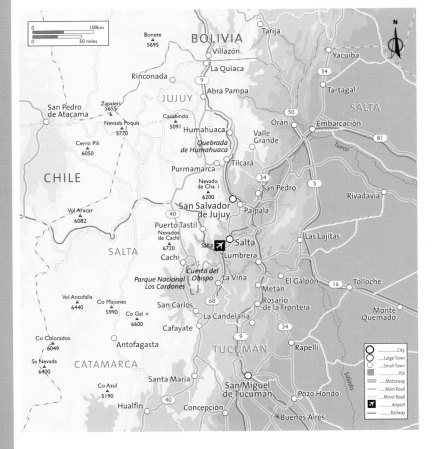

In 1544, with the Incas defeated, the Spanish discovered a rich vein of silver in the highlands of present-day Bolivia. A new city, Potosí, quickly grew up around the mines, and became the largest in the western hemisphere. Huge quantities of silver were shipped overland to the powerful Viceroy of Lima. The people around Salta prospered too, through the sale of strong pack animals to the miners. On the side, silver flowed from the mines south to Salta, in return for hardware and foodstuffs – a trade that was illegal under the bureaucratic rules of the Spanish Crown. The hardware for the mines came from Buenos Aires, where much of the silver ended up. Needless to say, this too was frowned upon.

Those days have left a lasting legacy here. Rapidly accumulating great wealth, horse breeders in Salta were able to refine and perfect their equine stock. The best gauchos were attracted north, and the area gained a reputation for excellence in horsemanship that still holds true today. Master silversmiths, leather-workers and weavers also prospered as the nouveau-riche gauchos demanded the finest saddles, bridles and ponchos that money could buy.

This was the root of Argentina's master crafts, and is a large part of what makes Salta special today. The wines, cuisine and people exude a colourful confidence, borne of centuries of interaction with other Andean peoples, and this is aptly reflected in Argentina's grand canyons – the *quebradas* of Cafayate and Humahuaca – with their intense artistic forms.

Red rock stacks soar skywards from the floor of Salta's desert

THE HISTORIC CITY OF SALTA

Founded in 1582, Salta is one of the prettiest colonial cities in the whole of South America. It doesn't have the modern European feel of other Argentine cities, but feels more like a provincial capital of Bolivia or Peru. While Buenos Aires has embraced Irish, Italian and British customs to become the cosmopolitan centre it is today, it sometimes feels like Salta's clocks stopped in 1810, with the end of Spanish rule.

Plaza 9 de Julio

A good place to start your exploration is the city's main square, named after the day in 1816 when Argentina formally declared its independence. Dotted around are shops offering the

Iglesia San Francisco's bell tower

fine work of locally based artisans such as Bertero the silversmith (*workshop at Los Parrales 1002. Tel: (0387) 439 9422*). Opposite the cathedral, on the south side of the plaza is the whitewashed cabildo, the full-length of its façade shaded by ornate arched verandas. Its current incarnation dates from 1783 and houses the **Museo Histórico del Norte** – an interesting retrospective of life in the region over the centuries. *Caseros 549. Tel: (0387) 421 5340. Open: Tue–Sat 9.30am–1:30pm & 3.30–8.30pm, Sun 9.30am–1.30pm. Admission charge.*

Museo de Arqueología de Alta Montaña (MAAM)

The Museum of High Mountain Archaeology contains, somewhat disconcertingly, the well-preserved bodies of a girl (aged 6), boy (7) and 'maiden' (15) who were sacrificed by the Incas on the summit of Volcán Llullaillaco. Their frozen forms were discovered in 1999, along with the priceless gold and silver artefacts that were intended, like their lives, as gifts to the gods. Scientists have established that, at some point after her death, the six-year old was struck by lightning on the mountaintop. The museum is thoroughly engaging and has rapidly become one of the city's main attractions.
Mitre 77. Tel: (0387) 437 0499. www.maam.org.ar. Open: Tue–Sun 9am–1pm & 4–9pm. Admission charge.

Parque San Martín and Cerro San Bernardo (1,454m/4,770ft)

Head west from the main square to Parque San Martín, a pleasant green space with an ornamental lake. For a great view of the city, you can take the *teleferico* (cable car) up to the summit of San Bernardo, where there are some formal gardens and a new restaurant. *San Martín esq. Yrigoyen. Tel: (0387) 431 0641. Open: 9am–6.45pm.*

Religious riches

The **Iglesia Catedral** (*Espana 537*) is spectacularly lit in the evening, and adds to the atmosphere of the main square, but its brilliance is outshone by the **Iglesia San Francisco** (*Córdoba 33*). The church's five-tiered belfry rises 53m (174ft) into the air, dwarfing everything around it, and houses a bell forged from war-of-independence cannons. The **Convento de San Bernardo** (*Caseros 73*) is a spartan white edifice, dating from 1625. It is still occupied by nuns, so visitors can only see it from the outside. *All churches have irregular opening hours, free admission.*

Tren a las Nubes (Train to the Clouds)

Currently undergoing restoration, this is a spectacular 220-km (137-mile) rail journey through plunging valleys connected by tunnels and crossed by dizzying viaducts, including La Polvorilla at 4,200m (13,780ft) above sea level. If the website (*www.trenalasnubes.com.ar*) is back online during your stay, the train should be too – don't miss it.

The city of Salta from San Bernardo's sky gardens

Tour: Changing plains – south of the city

Southwest of Salta, the road rises towards Cachi in a hair-raising but beautiful drive that winds around the steep hillside. From Cachi, Ruta 40 runs south and down to a cluster of bodegas around the small colonial town of Cafayate, where dedicated artisans take life at their own pace. Ruta 40 continues south to El Calafate (even Argentinians get the two mixed up) but Ruta 68 leads north from Cafayate – where the colourful rock formations of the Quebrada de Cafayate are a visual feast.

Cachi

If you take the bus from Salta, be prepared for some anxious moments as the driver blithely swings the old crate around the hairpin bends. The locals named this steep climb La Cuesta del Obisbo (the Bishop's Slope) after a senior clergymen travelling from Salta to Cachi was overtaken by nightfall and had to spend the night halfway up. The village itself is a picture postcard of white buildings constructed from *adobe* (mud) bricks. Originally a *hacienda* (an estate or huge ranch), it was then donated to the church, which built the Iglesia San José in 1796 and parcelled off the rest for locals to build homes upon.

Cafayate

Although Mendoza is the wine capital of Argentina, Cafayate is catching up fast. The dry climate here is perfect for production of the Torrontés grape, among others. **Bodega La Rosa**, on the

northern edge of town, is one of the best wineries, with an enthusiastic hostess who wants to share her love of cookery, wine and the countryside. The grand colonial house at its centre is a great place to spend a night or two, combining wine tasting with horse riding and relaxing.
Ruta 40 s/n. Tel: (03868) 421 139/201. www.micheltorino.com.ar.

Parque Nacional Los Cardones

This park protects the Cardon, a species of cactus that looks like every child's drawing of the plant. Enormous, green and prickly, its 10cm (4-inch) thorns reduce evaporation in the arid climate, and provide protection from hungry animals. Cardon wood has traditionally been used for furniture, roof beams, toys and even musical instruments, although the trees in the park are all protected.

In terms of animal life, guanacos are common in the park, travelling in herds of 10 to 20, but other fauna can be difficult to spot. Pumas and grey foxes are both here, as are the bellied opossum (a smallish armadillo) and more than 100 bird species, including falcons and the Andean condor.

Quebrada de Cafayate

The elements have creatively exposed rich rainbows and towering sculptures in the sandstone of this extraordinary landscape, between Cafayate and Salta to the north. The paved road through the desert canyon passes the dizzying formations of Los Castillos (castles),

El Obelisco (obelisk) and the undisputed highlight, La Garganta del Diablo (devil's throat), all of them so aptly named that they are easily recognisable. Rather than taking one of the perfunctory tours, consider hiring a car in Salta; or hire a bicycle there, take it on the bus to Cafayate, then cycle back. It is a wonderful journey of 183km (114 miles), with pretty colonial towns and bodegas along the way, but common-sense precautions are required: don't travel alone and bring plenty of water and food in case of accidents or delays.

Chillies left out to dry in the sun near Cafayate

Tour: Quebrada de Humahuaca

Jujuy is the starting point of this tour, which lasts two days and is a 260-km (161-mile) round trip. The highlight is the World Heritage Site of Quebrada de Humahuaca, a huge gorge cut deep into the desert countryside, which is best seen out of the heat of the midday sun. It is possible to make this trip by public bus or as part of a tour (sit on the right for the best views), but hiring a car gives you more freedom. The route follows an old colonial trade route from the Andes to the plains, taking in various scenic delights along the way. Those in a hurry can visit Quebrada de Humahuaca in a day from either Salta or Jujuy.

1 San Salvador de Jujuy

Normally known simply as Jujuy, the city's colonial heart has, in recent years, been overwhelmed by modern buildings. In its centre, the interiors of both the Cathedral and **Capilla de Santa Bárbara** owe much to the Peruvian Cusco School of Art, while the cabildo and **Casa de Gobierno** (Government House)

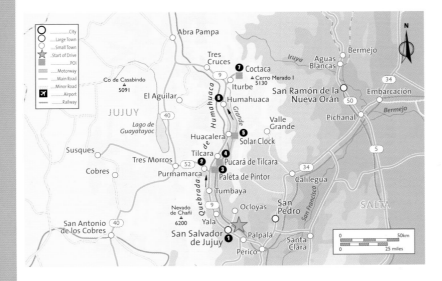

are two key buildings of historical note.
From Jujuy, take Ruta 9 north. Turn west
onto Ruta 52 to Purmamarca, which is
65km (40 miles) from Jujuy and clearly
signposted.

2 Purmamarca

From the pretty main plaza in the
village of Purmamarca, a 3-km (2-mile)
circuit, the Paseo de Siete Colores leads
to the **Cerro de Siete Colores** (Hill of
Seven Colours). It's a gravel road that
can be driven or walked.
Continue north for 12km (7¹/₂ miles) on
Ruta 9.

3 The Paleta de Pintor

The 'Painter's Palette', this stretches up
behind the small settlements east of the
road. It is easy to imagine some
supernatural being toying with his
earthy palette of reds, browns, ambers
and yellows before carefully sculpting
and colouring the astonishing forms
that meet the eye.
Continue north for 6km (3¹/₂ miles),
through Maimara and onto Tilcara.

4 Tilcara

This is a centre for artisans, housing a
museum of archaeology and another of
regional painting. Just south of the
village are the remains of **Pucará de**
Tilcara, a pre-Columbian fort
complex constructed by the
indigenous people and faithfully
rebuilt in the 1950s.
Continue north for 16km (10 miles)
to Huacalera.

5 Huacalera

Passing though the farming village of
Huacalera, look out for the 50-m
(164-ft) wide **solar clock** on the left-
hand side of the road, which marks
the progress of the Tropic of
Capricorn.
The village of Humahuaca, after which
the valley is named, is 30km (18¹/₂ miles)
north along the same road.

6 Humahuaca

The buildings here are almost all
dazzlingly white, a collection of
postcard-pretty *adobe* (mud) houses
and churches, lining well-maintained
cobbled streets. Don't miss the
handicrafts market and the performing
clock tower. Visitors with time should
spend the night here and enjoy some
local hospitality – a good choice is the
Posada el Sol *(Medalla Milagrosa s/n.*
Tel: (03887) 421 466.
www.posadaelsol.com.ar) just over the
Río Grande *bridge.*
In the village, ask a taxi driver, or
friendly local, to take you along the
10-km (6-mile) dirt track to the **pre-**
Columbian ruins at Coctaca.

7 Coctaca

Here, the remains of an ancient
settlement can still be seen in the dry
stone agricultural terracing that was the
hallmark of Inca civilisation.
It is a 130-km (81-mile) drive back to
Jujuy. Before you set off the next day,
why not go horse riding in the morning –
just ask at the Posada.

Argentina's master crafts

The two unforgiving bands of black on the traditional Saltese poncho symbolise the death of local Independence fighter, Güemes; the deep red background denotes the lost blood of his soldiers. The flamboyant poncho – like the Scottish hunting kilt from which it is thought to derive – was once used in war, but is now worn for warmth and as a declaration of clan. The archetypal souvenir from Salta is typical of Argentina's craftsmanship – culturally resonant, decorative and yet eminently practical.

Artists' enclaves

Some claim Salta as the cradle of Argentine crafts, because official records show the country's first craft market opened here in 1968. Whatever the facts, up and down the land committed artisans hammer out silver, relentlessly drive looms and keenly stitch leather. San Antonio de Areco is generally recognised as the capital of the artisan movement, with its open workshops that form living museums, but many of its resident craftsmen have their roots in the north.

As well as urban enclaves, there are hundreds of remote communities producing extraordinary work, often inspired by the spectacular landscape.

Fine leather rope work

Unquestionable quality

The country's artisans are living examples of a vibrant craft movement. Their products are built to last, not one, but several lifetimes and display a loving, rather than a solemn, reverence for their past and their future. For many, their work is both a matter of family tradition and an expression of their deepest creative urges, in the tradition of pure 'art'. These pieces are absolutely 'authentic' in that they are deeply rooted in the locale and the craftsperson. Most of what is produced is unique and of the highest quality – in terms of material, skill of the creator and attention to detail.

Fashioned from the land

Like any good artist, Argentina's craftspeople make good use of the materials available to them. Hide and horn are obvious choices in 'cow country', fashioned into everything from stylish handbags to exquisite utensils. Local animal hair is woven so that cold natives can wrap up in cheerfully coloured llama and sheep wool ponchos, textiles and blankets. Particularly in the north, where thick forests are all around, woodcarving comes into its own. Here, the Wichi people skilfully whittle coloured local timber to make utensils and ornaments in charming animal shapes.

Solid silver Creole 'Arequro' stirrup

Fair trade

Artisanal shopping means that rather than just bringing home a beautiful souvenir, you can reinvest in the art – and the heart – of the country. Expect to pay for the real thing – pieces created by hand rather than machine are costly – and try to put your money straight, or as near as possible, into the pocket of the artist. Boutiques in Buenos Aires offering crafts from around the country may appeal to those short of time, but ask yourself how many of your pesos go to the creator. Try instead to buy direct from the artist – in the marketplace, at craft fairs, from the workshop, or through groups such as Shinkal (*www.shinkal.com*), a fair trade organisation that represents individual Argentine artists online worldwide.

Getting away from it all

In Argentina, where land and sky extends as far as the eye can see, it is almost impossible to feel boxed in. The airy plains of the pampas are only an hour's drive from the capital. Hillside villages and historic Jesuit settlements spread out from the city of Córdoba. Mendoza is surrounded by fine vineyards, and all roads from Salta lead to dramatic multicoloured ravines and mountains. Whether it's El Calafate with its nearby glacial ice fields or Bariloche – a populous hub in a tranquil sea of lakes and mountains – getting away from it all is easy here.

All of the above destinations have been covered in previous chapters, but this section offers some carefully selected suggestions for really getting away from it all. Some can be squeezed in when you have just a day or two to spare, while others might need a week or more – Antarctica, in particular, is a big commitment, not least financially. For those with plenty of time, don't be afraid to stick a pin in the map and head where fate decrees. In seemingly ordinary villages and towns, where people rarely see tourists of any nationality, the visitor gets a real sense of Argentinean values; the hospitality, easygoing nature and sense of fun of the locals will leave you with unforgettable memories.

Aconcagua: Roof of the Americas

West of Mendoza, an ancient trail leads through the Andes to Chilean territory. Along the way is Cerro Aconcagua which, at 6,962m (22,841ft) high, is the highest mountain in the western hemisphere. It dwarfs anything in Europe – you could stack Ben Nevis (Britain's highest peak) on top of Mont Blanc (Europe's) and still be short of the summit by almost a kilometre. It is one of the most challenging climbs anywhere in the world, but even hiking in the foothills (more than 3,000m/9,843ft above sea level) is no picnic. Take it slowly to avoid altitude sickness and enjoy the splendid isolation of the rocky hillsides and snowy mountain passes.

Uspallata makes a good base for exploring this region, though the town itself is nothing much to speak of. Locals are proud that Hollywood heartthrob, Brad Pitt stayed here during the filming of *Seven Years in Tibet*, and the scenery close by is truly cinematic. The trail from Upsallata leads to a natural bridge used by the Incas, as they spread south in the final decades of their empire. Their crossing point,

Crossing point: Puente del Inca

Puente del Inca, was formed by mineral deposits from thermal springs and attracts adventurous tourists who are following in the conquerors' footsteps. The rocky formation is a blaze of copper in the brown and green hills. Further along the pass the small resort of Las Cuevas is dwarfed by the surrounding icy peaks, and visitors can hike in the Parque Provincial Aconcagua, where the wild land is frequently covered by fresh falls of snow.

Antarctica

Around three quarters of the ships going to 'the white continent' leave from the frontier city of Ushuaia. This makes it the ideal place to grab a last-minute half-price fare, which still means paying anything from US$3,000 (£1,500) for 9 to 14 days, plus a whacking 5 per cent surcharge for credit card payments. Your vessel could be anything from a rugged Russian icebreaker to a 'luxury' cruise ship (don't expect casinos and discos). Smaller boats can be uncomfortable in rough weather but allow you to get closer to the ice; also, because there is a limit to the number of people who can land on Antarctica at any one time, bigger ships with more than 100 passengers offer fewer opportunities for those all-important ice treks.

Ninety-eight per cent of the world's last great wilderness is covered in ice.

The icy lands of beautiful Antarctica

It is impractical to visit Antarctica in winter (when it is four times the size of Australia), and even in summer (November to March), temperatures hover between an icy −6ºC (21.2ºF) and a bone-chilling −10ºC (14ºF). What you will see depends on the time of your visit; from November to early December, the ice is just beginning to melt, but there are still some enormous icebergs floating around and penguins and other seabirds are beginning to mate. Mid-December to January is the warmest time, when days are long, chicks are hatching and fur seals are breeding. By February, the ice melt is well on its way, opening up new areas and increasing the chance of whale sightings.

Colonia del Sacramento

Time really does seem to have stood still in this lovely old Uruguayan town, just across the Río de la Plata from Buenos Aires. Portuguese settlers founded Colonia in 1680 (when Uruguay was part of their South American empire) and it is now a UNESCO World Heritage Site. The main focus for visitors is the compact Barrio Histórico (Old Town), where colonial houses draped with flowers line quiet, cobbled streets.

Wander around (or hire a bicycle – a popular option) with occasional stops in the inviting small cafés and craft shops that have been set up in elegant period mansions. At the centre, Plaza

Mayor is home to two museums whose settings are as interesting as their contents. The artefacts, weaponry and furniture in the Museo Portugués once belonged to the original settlers, while the quirky Museo Municipal displays decorative doorknobs and dead butterflies (*Open: 11am–5pm. Admission charge*).

Most visitors from Buenos Aires come on a day trip, crossing the estuary at 9am and returning at 7pm (*Tel: (011) 4316 6500. www.buquebus.com. One-hour trip by hydrofoil; three hours by regular ferry*) although two days allows more time for relaxing. Arrive early at the port, leaving plenty of time to clear customs. Travellers from western Europe, Canada, Australia and New Zealand don't need a visa (other nationals should check with their embassies) but passports are essential for all. Avoid summer weekends, when crowds from Buenos Aires descend on the small town, and hotels are more expensive, if not full.

La Feria de Mataderos

For a real taste of the gauchos' cowboy lifestyle, you need only travel to the western edge of the capital. Here, the Mataderos area of Buenos Aires hosts an atmospheric weekly fair of popular Argentine traditions and handicrafts. Gauchos compete in theatrical horseback games, racing each other up and down the sandy streets, while flamboyant folk dancers of all ages perform age-old set pieces in the square. As well as absorbing the visual spectacle, visitors can try their luck at *sapo* (tossing a coin into the mouth of a

Colonia's cobbled streets are a throwback to earlier days

metal frog) or humiliate themselves on the *palo enjabonado* (greasy pole).

Shoppers can lose themselves at the market where stalls sell leatherwear and maté gourds – and sometimes even horses – together with ceramics and decorative pieces, almost all at very reasonable prices. The food is another diversion, with delicious handmade *empanadas* (pasties), barbecued meat and traditional locro stew all there for the taking. All in all, it is a great day out, a real family event and an insight into a distinctly different way of life. Mataderos is a short taxi ride from the centre, or for local colour take a *collectivo* (public minibus) – see website for details.

Av. Lisandro de la Torre y Av. de los Corrales, Matatderos. Tel: (011) 4372 4836/4687 5602 (Sun only). www.feriademataderos.com.ar (Spanish only). Open: Jan–Mar Sat 6pm–noon, Apr–Dec Sun 11am–8pm. Cancelled if heavy rain.

Tigre

Less than 30km (19 miles) from the centre, Tigre is a great Buenos Aires getaway, at the confluence of the rivers Paraná and Uruguay, which between them drain large parts of Argentina, Brazil, Paraguay, Bolivia and Uruguay. Over centuries, river silt and sediment have formed hundreds of low-lying islands in this (the world's widest)

Tigre's riverside walks are a welcome retreat from Buenos Aires

Sailing boats on the Paraná River

estuary. With pleasant walks along the banks and over bridges, slow-moving canal boats and a scattering of bars and restaurants, Tigre feels more like a suburb of Amsterdam than Buenos Aires.

A highlight here is the Puerto de Frutas (*four blocks south of Estación Delta, 11am–7pm*), a bustling port market where the main offerings are no longer apples and bananas, but a variety of crafts produced by local artisans. Leather goods, and baskets and furniture made from willow reeds are the best buys, with the biggest selection available on Sunday.

At the port, there are some nice spots for a bite to eat, and pleasant canal tours lasting around 90 minutes leave from here. The boats cruise down the small Río Sarmiento, past attractive colonial mansions and newer riverside homes where the capital's wealthier citizens spend their weekends. None of the islands has roads, so you will see residents travelling around in water taxis, luxury launches and sailing boats, or even jet skis and kayaks. Children are likely to be fascinated by the hulking half-submerged shipwrecks that can be seen rusting away in the water.

Tigre can be reached by taxi from the city centre, but there are also two trains from there to Tigre's Estación Delta. The best of these is the Tren de la Costa (Coast Train), which leaves from the Olivos station. The other is a slow-stopping train that leaves from Retiro.

When to go

It is true to say that there isn't a bad time to visit Argentina – there are such huge variations of weather across the regions, that it is just a case of choosing which area suits you when. For most visitors, the summer months (October to April) are the best time for enjoying this part of the world, where the seasons are the reverse of those in the northern hemisphere. In winter, temperatures regularly fall below freezing and some attractions in the far south are closed. At the same time winter, of course, is when skiing comes into its own.

Unpredicatable weather

With the effects of climate change now presenting themselves on a daily basis, even less about the weather can be taken for granted. In Argentina, a solid week of rain can frequently interrupt an otherwise perfect summer by the lakes, or a heatwave can hit when it should be freezing. Some rules do still apply. Avoid trips to southern Patagonia and Tierra del Fuego in winter – it is far too cold. At the other end of the spectrum, cities in the north can be unbearable in summer, especially Buenos Aires and Córdoba.

Avoiding the crowds

It is advisable not to go on holiday at the same time as Argentineans, when accommodation, transport and

Aim to take in local festivals

restaurants are all full. At Christmas, thousands of *porteños* (residents of Buenos Aires) decamp from the capital and head in their droves to Mar del Plata and Bariloche, making it difficult for other visitors to get a look in. January is rather like August in Europe, when it seems that almost everyone is on holiday. During this month, as well as Easter and July, accommodation is often booked up.

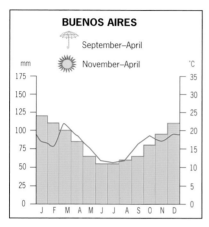

BUENOS AIRES

☂ September–April
☀ November–April

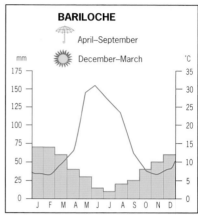

BARILOCHE

☂ April–September
☀ December–March

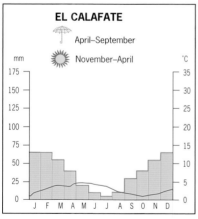

EL CALAFATE

☂ April–September
☀ November–April

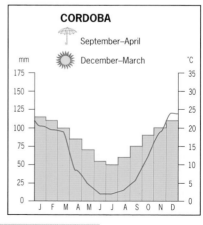

CORDOBA

☂ September–April
☀ December–March

WEATHER CONVERSION CHART

25.4mm = 1 inch

°F = 1.8 × °C + 32

Getting around

Before you start planning your internal travel arrangements, remember Argentina is almost 3,500km (2,175 miles) from north to south – the same distance from Canada to Spain to Canada. For a country of this size, the airline infrastructure is uncompetitive and woefully inadequate. Travel here can be exhausting. Be prepared for delays and cancellations and build some flexibility into your itinerary. Visitors who try to see everything on their first visit to Argentina often return home in need of another holiday – it pays to take it slowly and make the most of the locations you can sensibly manage.

By bus

In Argentina generally, and Patagonia in particular, almost the only way to get from place to place is by road, since flights from the major cities here are almost exclusively routed via Buenos Aires. Pretty much every town and city is linked by the bus network. For longer distance travel, choose between *cama* (like a business-class airline seat) and *semi-cama* (reclining seat) – both are comfortable services and don't stop as often as the cheaper services buses that

often have no air conditioning or onboard toilets.

Bus travel, whatever the class, costs only a fraction of the price of an airline ticket. Meals (usually snacks) are less common than they used to be, and the coffee served on 'luxury services' is not recommended; bring your own refreshments. Services between cities must often cross mountain ranges and plains with gravel tracks (especially Ruta 40 on the way to Bariloche), so avoid seats over the wheels, which can make for a bone-rattling journey. Longer bus rides are often scheduled overnight, but if you don't want to miss the scenery it is possible to make shorter hops by day.

By train

The golden age of train travel in Argentina went into decline almost from the moment the railways were nationalised. Fifty years of underinvestment means that only the

Buses are cheap and plentiful

Internal flights are pricey and prone to delays

province of Buenos Aires is served by any real network. Trains leave from Retiro station to Tigre and the northern suburbs, from Constitución to the beaches south of Buenos Aires, and from Once to the suburbs southwest of the city. Le Tren a las Nubes (the Train to the Clouds) (*see p113*) is not currently running, but the fascinating Old Patagonian Express, known here as La Trochita, is a narrow-gauge steam train still operating in Southern Patagonia (*www.latrochita.org.ar*).

For up-to-date details of bus, train and ferry services consult the *Thomas Cook Overseas Timetable*, published bi-monthly. It is available to buy in the UK at some stations, in Thomas Cook branches, by phoning *01733 416477* or online at *www.thomascookpublishing.com*

By air

The company Aerolíneas Argentinas (*www.aerolineas.com.ar*) has established something close to a monopoly on internal air travel. It gobbled up the former routes of LAPA (which went bankrupt in 2003) and Southern Winds, which closed after a major cocaine bust. It is supposedly the national airline, but is actually Spanish-owned. Aerolíneas doubled prices for foreigners in 2006, and their monopoly allows them to route virtually all flights via Buenos Aires. If a flight is cancelled, or delayed, don't expect compensation.

Lan (*www.lan.com*) is the only real alternative, but they have fewer flights, and if your flight is cancelled, you may have to wait days for the next one. The whole system is something of a national disgrace; Argentineans just raise their eyebrows at the mention of it. A good travel agent is essential, since they can often find seats when none are available on the web; Erna Rosenfeld (*Florida 470, Suite 406, Buenos Aires. Tel: (011) 4322 8147. www.travelsur.net*) is one of the best.

From Buenos Aires, most internal flights leave from Aeroparque Jorge Newbery (*www.aa2000.com.ar*), a basic airport with few facilities, but only a 20-minute drive from the centre.

By boat

Regular ferry services operate from BA across the Río Plata estuary to Colonia in Uruguay, while Ushuaia in Tierra del Fuego is the departure point for the Antarctic, Patagonian coast and Falkland Islands cruises (*see pp70–71*).

By bicycle

In the almost totally flat pampas, you will see plenty of farmers (when they are not on horseback) riding around on bicycles, and in a scenic town like San Antonio de Areco this is a great option; contact Patricia Jacovella for hire (*Tel: (02326) 453 674*). Even in the busy capital, travelling by bike is a good option as the streets are wide and flat, and car drivers, despite being generally oblivious to the rules of the road, are courteous to cyclists (*see p163*).

By car

All the usual international car hire firms operate in Argentina, from airports and city centre locations. In Buenos Aires, try:

Alamo Carlos Pellegrini 1175.
Tel: (011) 4322 3320.
Avis Cerrito 1527. *Tel: (011) 4326 5542.*
Budget Av. Leandro N Alem 1110.
Tel: (011) 4311 7788.
Dollar M T de Alvear 449.
Tel: (011) 4315 8800.
Hertz Paraguay 1138.
Tel: (011) 4816 8001.
Thrifty Carlos Pellegrini 1576.
Tel: (011) 4326 0418.

All traffic drives on the right, seat belts are compulsory, and drivers must be 18 years or older.

Leaving Ushuaia in Tierra del Fuego on a South Atlantic cruise

By taxi

In all cities, taxis are cheap and readily available on the street. Make sure the meter is working before you travel and, if it is a long distance, ask the driver to clearly confirm the price beforehand. If you take a taxi from a large hotel, you will pay a minimum fare regardless of where you are going. A *remis* is similar to a taxi but can only be booked by telephone. Ask the price when you book. Watch out for unscrupulous drivers, particularly at the airports and late at night (*see p159*).

Access for travellers with disabilities

More advanced than many of its neighbours, there has been disabled rights legislation in Argentina since 1982, and in 2002 laws were passed to make tourist facilities fully accessible to travellers with disabilities as well.

In Buenos Aires and other major destinations, most good hotels have ramps or handrails, together with lifts. New hotels usually have at least one or two rooms with fully accessible facilities, but check in advance. In BA, Transpdisc (*Tel: (011) 4993 9883. www.transpdisc.com.ar*) is a reputable firm offering wheelchair-accessible taxis and city tours. Decthird (*Tel: (011) 4182 5469. www.decthird.com*) is a specialist tour company offering customised trips further afield. Access Able is a good website with general advice. *www.access-able.com*

Yellow-top taxis are the fastest way to get around Buenos Aires

Accommodation

Crucially for foreign travellers, the rating system of one to five stars rarely matches international standards, particularly in terms of service. Accommodation is best judged on criteria such as charm and cuisine, rather than numbers of restaurants or parking facilities. This is particularly true of Argentina's most memorable lodgings – estancias, desirable because of their location, activities and history and the unique opportunity to get a glimpse of rural Argentine life. In this guide, independent, owner-operated establishments, which tend to offer more personal service and local atmosphere, have been selected wherever possible.

Unfortunately, many of the country's 'design' or boutique hotels are all shine and no service. While the décor may feature real wood and minimalist bathrooms, attention to detail and staff competency tend to be more corner cutting than cutting edge. The 'designer' establishments mentioned in this guide are the happy exception. Otherwise, anyone seeking style is advised to look for the conservative sort: opt for a traditional hotel that more than makes up for what it lacks in cool chic with good old-fashioned charm and service.

Peso pinching

Watch out for expensive imports such as Scotch whisky or French mineral water, which can push up your bar or room service bill by as much as your room charge for a night. In higher end hotels, prices normally include breakfast but not the 21 per cent sales tax, which dramatically raises the room rate. Hotels that quote in US dollars are clearly aimed at foreign tourists and are usually considerably more costly than establishments geared to locals;

WHAT'S IN A NAME?

Apartamentos (apartments) – mostly in Buenos Aires – are an excellent alternative to hotels, particularly for those with children, offering better prices and facilities, such as kitchens and more space.

Cabanitas (cabins) may be anything from a rustic log cabin to a luxury lodge in a resort, often with a kitchen and with space enough for a family.

Hosterías (usually budget- to mid-range hotels) are not hostels, despite their name, and can even be very luxurious, such as Hostería Isla Victoria in the Lake District (*see p168*).

Telos (love hotels), also called *alberges transitorios* (transitory hotels) are usually rented by the hour and bookings cannot usually be taken.

Charming luxury cabins dot the shores of Patagonia's Lake District

foreigners are sometimes even charged a higher price. Having chosen your accommodation, do consider upgrading. Just a little more money can often get you a much better room – perhaps a suite with a view and even a Jacuzzi. Organised tours and services from large, tourist hotels can be poor value for money; often the same excursions or better can be found locally and purchased directly from the provider at a fraction of the price.

Love hotels

Telos (love hotels) are a practical, even romantic, response to local living conditions. For couples that live with their extended families, *telos* offer complete privacy, and can be a great diversion for tourists, too. They don't advertise, rarely have a sign, and many travellers don't even know they exist. *Telos* range from seedy motels to luxurious mansions with extravagant themes that are frequented by film stars and politicians alike.

Estancias

'Life on an estancia *is one of the freest, and most enjoyable perhaps, on the face of the earth... the land bounded in every direction only by the bright blue vault of heaven, the immense herds and flocks, the wealth that grows unbidden... the free and hospitable welcome and the vast silence.'*
E W White, *Tales from Silverland* (1881)

Estancia literally means ranch, but could be anything from a rustic shack to a lavish Italianate palace. Many of the buildings in the rich pampas were

Relax on a luxury *estancia*

once great estates, filled with fine European furniture by their wealthy owners. In contrast, Patagonian *estancias* have always been struggling farmhouses, built when the government gave away large areas of mostly barren land as a way of populating the deserted region more than 100 years ago.

In recent years, economic difficulties have forced owners in all regions to open their doors to tourists, and create something akin to English country hotels – but with a level of service that would put many of those establishments to shame. As well as offering a piece of history, they provide an insight into the local way of life and luxury at a very affordable price. The historic Jesuit *estancias* around Córdoba are something quite different – these are now museums, offering daily sightseeing tours, but certainly not meals or lodgings.

Historic houses
For good or bad, the fate of *estancias* is linked to the fate of the country as a whole. When the economy boomed on the back of beef and wool exports, the *estancias* prospered. In lean times (and there have been

On the best *estancias*, owners make time for their guests

plenty), the great ranches teetered on the edge of bankruptcy, and often fell over the edge. According to some estimates, as many as half of the *estancias* in the province of Santa Cruz have been deserted due to financial hardship. At the same time, American investors have been diving into the huge pool of land that is southern Patagonia, buying enormous tracts of wilderness and grand estancias. The Bush family and former CNN boss Ted Turner are now bona fide Patagonian *caudillos* (landowners).

Down at the ranch

The best *estancias* are managed day-to-day by their owners, who might well live in a smaller cottage, giving the main house over to guests. Their unrelenting hospitality never ceases to amaze, but choose your establishment carefully; an absent or uninterested owner can make the experience dull, or even miserable. It cannot be emphasised enough that poor hospitality will ruin your stay, while the real thing will provide lifelong happy memories.

Most *estancias* accommodate between 10 and 20 people, providing a range of accommodation and serving at least one *asado* (barbecue) daily. Contact with the outside world is often by radio only (or satellite internet). It is also possible to visit an *estancia* on a *día del campo* (day in the country), having lunch, tea and going horse riding or exploring the grounds. Many establishments now have swimming pools and are set up for relaxation as much as active tourism.

Food and drink

There are few surprises on Argentine menus. Expect excellent meat, of course, lots of fresh salads, pasta and maybe pizza and fish, which means there are usually at least several dishes to suit vegetarians and children. Although haute and fusion cuisines do make an appearance in some of the cities' more fashionable restaurants, they tend to be disappointing. Eating establishments from old school confiterías *(cafés) to trendy* resto-bars *(restaurant-bars) sometimes lack atmosphere when compared to Europe or the US; look out for traditional* parrillas *(grills) full of happy locals, serving roasted meat and other dishes, and you won't go far wrong.*

Many Argentineans eat four meals a day. *Desayuno* (breakfast) for a local is often bread and pastries, although in most tourist hotels, eggs and fresh fruit are also served. *Almuerzo* (lunch) is normally light, although meat may be eaten then, too. Afternoon tea is still a daily ritual in the estancias, but has been replaced by coffee and cake or a drink and *picadas* (nibbles, such as olives or peanuts) after work in urban areas.

Service is usually friendly but very relaxed, meaning that meal times often last for hours. Argentineans eat dinner late, usually after 10pm; this can cause difficulties if travelling with children, as many restaurants don't open until 8pm. The advantage is that it is usually possible to get a decent table at even at the most popular restaurant if you eat at 8pm or 9pm. When you receive *la cuenta* (the bill) and hand over your cash, hold back from saying '*gracias*' immediately as this can be taken as a sign that you don't want change. Don't, however, forget to leave a *propina* (tip) of 10–15 per cent, unless there was a problem with the meal; waiting staff rely on tips to supplement their income.

Big on beef

The world famous Argentine *carne* (beef) is usually of the highest quality and *asados* (barbecues) are perhaps even more popular here than in Australia. Steaks tend to be overcooked by western standards – if you like a little colour in your cut, ask for it *a punto* (medium) or *jugoso* (rare). Don't expect potatoes or vegetables with your meat; it is more likely to come with salad, although side dishes can be ordered separately. *Chimichurri* is a delicious sauce of oil, garlic and

Old-school restaurants offer the best cuisine and service to match

herbs that makes a good accompaniment and is much more common than mustard or ketchup.

The two most popular beef cuts are *bife de chorizo* (rump or sirloin steak) and *bife de lomo* (tenderloin or filet mignon), usually cooked *a la paprilla* (on hot coals) and sometimes spit roast over a fire. A *parrillada* (mixed grill) may also include *morcilla* (blood sausage), *cerdo* (pork) and *chuletas* (chops). *Pollo* (pronounced 'po-jo'), and, less often, *pato* (duck), along with *milanesa* (thin breaded and fried beef

or chicken) are other options for carnivores. Travel south to Patagonia and you will find local *cordero* (lamb) replacing steaks on many menus, while in the northwest, goat and llama may make an appearance on the menu.

Fast food

It is easy to eat *al paso* (fast food – literally 'on the move') at excellent *rotiserías* (delicatessens) packed with Italian fare, functional *lanches* (snack bars), or indeed anywhere serving *minutes* (snacks). *Empanadas* are delicious pasties found on almost every street corner. They are filled with *carne* (beef), *pollo* (chicken), *queso* (cheese) *jamón* (ham), and sometimes vegetables. Drinks are rarely served without *picadas* (nibbles), such as *aceitunas* (olives).

Drink up

When it comes to alcohol in Argentina, it pays to follow the old adage, 'When in Rome…' Excellent national champagne can be had for a song, and native spirits, while sometimes a bit rough around the edges, are a bargain compared to the highly inflated prices of imported brands. The Argentine beer, *Quilmes*, will please most palates,

with Brazilian Brahma also available.

Local wines are predictably good and reasonably priced, and even some of the cheapest bottles are very drinkable (*see pp96–7*). Argentina is justly famous for its full-bodied *tinto* (red wine) but don't miss a chance to try one of the local white wines, particularly the Sauvignon Blanc and Chardonnay that is coming out of Mendoza and some of the lesser-known vineyards further north. House wines, at least, are sold by the glass; ask for '*una copa de...*' if you don't want a full bottle.

Argentina is a nation of coffee drinkers. *Café* (coffee) *con leche* (with milk) and *cafetico* (espresso, literally 'a little coffee') can be found on almost

Hot-dogs for sale in Plaza de Mayo, Buenos Aires

MENU DECODER: A TO Z

a la plancha	grilled
al vapor	steamed
arroz	rice
berenja	aubergine
cacahuete	nuts
calamares	squid
camarones	prawns
ensalada	salad
fruta	fruit
huevo	egg
jamón crudo	prosciutto
lenguado	sole
manteca	butter
mariscos	shellfish
mejillones	mussels
palta	avocado
pan	bread
papas	potato
papas fritas	chips
pescado	fish
trucha	trout
zanahoria	carrot

every street corner. Coffee houses and smarter restaurants are likely to offer cappuccinos as well as delicious *submarinos* (a bar of chocolate dipped into hot milk). *Maté* is a local brew of herb tea served in a gourd with a *bombilla* (silver straw) and much favoured by the gauchos. It is drunk almost addictively throughout the country, although you won't find it in restaurants. Black tea is not of good quality, and you will normally have to ask for milk as it rarely comes as standard.

Agua mineral sin/con gas (water still/carbonated) can be bought in small and large bottles just about anywhere, as can *refrescos* (carbonated drinks), both international and local. *Licuados* are milk shakes of various flavours; *jugos* (fruit juices) are a healthy alternative.

Sweet teeth

Dulces (sweet things) are often eaten for breakfast and many children will delight in being served chocolate cake, *medialunas* (small, sweet croissants), tarts and pastries for their first meal of the day. *Alfajores* are biscuits filled with anything from chocolate to fruit, and are sold in large numbers in shops and cafés from morning to night throughout the country. Caramelised milk, known as *dulce de leche*, is something of a national dish and a key ingredient of most Argentine desserts. *Tortas* (tarts) and *arroz con leche* (rice pudding) are two of the most popular ways to round off a meal.

A submarino goes down well, instead of coffee or dessert

Entertainment

Buenos Aires, and, to a much lesser degree, other cities such as Córdoba and Mendoza, have a rich cultural scene. Theatre, ballet and opera performances are world class and often held in historic venues that are tourist destinations in their own right. The most obvious example of this is the Teatro Colón (see p29) with its outstanding acoustics and long tradition of hosting the biggest names in classical entertainment.

Nightlife

Nightlife starts late – very late. With most locals still at dinner when the clocks strike twelve, clubs and dancing venues usually don't get going until 2am, and are still sweeping out stragglers long past sunrise. Bars, clubs and shows (known as *espectáculos*, and rather imaginatively often translated as

The drama of tango

'spectacles') change all the time, though of course the best places have staying power. In the capital, pick up a free copy of *Buenos Aires Day and Night* for current listings for concerts – both classical and pop, as well as tango performances.

No smoking

The legendary *milongas* (tango clubs) of Buenos Aires are smoky no more. In October 2006, a city law banned smoking in all public spaces under 100sq m (1,076sq ft). In premises larger than that, the proprietor can choose to have a smoking area, or keep it all smoke-free. Outside of the capital, there are different smoking laws, depending on the province. Most cities permit smoking in all public places, but that looks set to change, with Argentina considering a country-wide ban.

The world of tango

In Buenos Aires, tango night is every night, with an overwhelming variety of

The Teatro Colón is the hub of high culture in Buenos Aires

shows and dance venues to choose from, usually with live orchestras. There are intimate, often more authentic venues and larger, glitzy performances that are usually aimed at tourists. The more commercialised operations offer dinner with or before the show, and the food is definitely not the main event; these places aim to provide a visual spectacle for foreign tourists.

For those who want to tango, *milongas* are the place to go. Often classes are on offer before the actual tango club opens, and there are private teachers and tango schools throughout the city. Learning the tango is not just about getting to know the moves, but the strict etiquette of the dance, too. Women may be invited to dance simply by *cabeceo* (a subtle movement involving direct eye contact, and a slight inclination of the head), or using a more forthright request. An answer can be given in the same way. A *cortina* (curtain) of non-tango music is played between each *tanda* (a group of songs, usually between three and five); this is the time to change partners and have a drink, but definitely *not* to dance.

There is no such thing as a simple tango any more. Tango Nuevo uses elements of jazz and classical music, while Neotango, its most recent mutation, incorporates non-tango dance moves and tracks. Electronic tango is perhaps the most startling phenomenon; it combines the use of traditional instruments with synthesizers.

Shopping

Don't come to Argentina expecting great bargains. The devaluation of the peso in 2002 had tourists scrambling here, but prices have levelled out and many outlets are now broadly comparable with Europe or the USA. Small shops close for a siesta – but shopping centres, boutiques and those in tourist areas stay open late into the evening. Fashion-hunters here have always been well catered for – provided they can squeeze into a size zero. A law was passed in 2006 requiring shops in BA to carry a full range of sizes in an attempt to combat the nation's alarming rate of anorexia, which is one of the highest in the world.

Avoid bland shopping centres, such as the much touted Galerías Pacifico in Buenos Aires. They are largely uninspiring, but tolerable if you have something specific in mind. Head to smaller shops and boutiques, where special finds await; Palermo in the capital provides particularly rich pickings. Don't miss the chance to visit a local *feria* (fair). On Sundays, San Telmo's feria is an antiques extravaganza, although the prices may restrict many to window-shopping (*see p30*).

Take-away Argentina: good buys

Leather goods, such as bags, shoes, jackets and belts are good value, but check the quality first – particularly of fastenings. Colourful textiles and ponchos, especially those from Salta, make practical souvenirs and gifts. Gaucho gear is found all over Argentina, while silver goods, from jewellery to goblets, are sparkling stand-outs. Big photographic books on estancias, wildlife, gauchos, food, wine and handicrafts are often of a high standard. Usually available in English, titles bought in the country are cheaper than at home, but still pricey.

Some remote shops are living museums

Homemade jams and marmalades are good buys in Córdoba

Preserves made in Córdoba and chocolates from Bariloche make good, simple gifts, but check the contents against your home country's foodstuff import laws. Buying bottles, or even crate-loads of Argentine wine may be decidedly more decadent, but with many bodegas providing packaging for export, and companies such as Terroir (*www.terroir.com.ar*) shipping bottles to anywhere in the world, there is little reason not to indulge.

The way to shop

Indigenous populations offer a rich source of locally made products (*see pp118–19*). When buying handicrafts try, wherever possible, to buy direct from the source; otherwise look out for *Comercio Justo* (Fair Trade) operations. **Pasion Argentina** (*www.pasion-argentina.com.ar*) is a pioneer in this sector, helping indigenous women to produce furniture, textiles and fashions that benefit local communities. Their main shop is in Buenos Aires (*Emilio Ravignani 1780*) but they have outlets in the US and Europe, too. **Tierra Adentro** (*www.tierraadentro.info*) is another ethical business, and sells items that embody the spirit of the Argentine aborigines, from two boutiques in the capital.

TAX-FREE SHOPPING

Some shops in Argentina offer non-citizens a refund of the 21 per cent sales tax (minus an administration fee) paid on goods costing more than 70 pesos. Look for the Tax-Free shopping sign or consult *www.globalrefund.com* and its searchable shop locator. At the time of purchase you will be given a Global Refund certificate. This, along with the receipt and the goods bought, must then be presented to customs before check-in, with a refund issued at the 'Tax Free' kiosk after passport control. Make sure to leave enough time before your flight to do this.

Sport and leisure

From its deepest valleys to its highest peaks, Argentina's spectacular, empty landscapes invite active participation. Whether you want to approach your chosen activity at a leisurely trot, or let go of the reins on a fifth-gear gallop, there is something for everyone. Enthusiasts can indulge their favourite pastime during extended packages offered by tour agencies, but most of the activities below can also be tasted in a day. For safety's sake, pick a reputable company and, for the future of the planet, seek one that shows a real concern for the environment; the 'ecotourism' label is often used here as little more than a marketing tool.

Canoeing and kayaking

Still lakes and fast-flowing rivers buoy contented canoeists and kayakers through the scenic backdrop that is Argentina. South of Bariloche, Extremo Sur (*see p169*) offers good value trips, while Rios Andinos (*see p170*) operates in the Andean foothills

Rafting in Mendoza (above) or the Lake District is world class

near Mendoza. For a bit of a twist, canyon-sliding is a rollercoaster of a ride, plunging into deep canyons, shooting through waterfalls and coming up for air on tranquil pools, possible on the Azul River in El Bolsón.

Cycling and mountain biking

Travelling on two wheels is very popular in Argentina, with the country perhaps more geared up to transport by bicycle than any other in South America. Bikes are available for hire in most cities and many smaller towns and villages for local exploration. More extensive trips can be taken through mountains and even across the Andes.

Football

Porteños of all ages long for another Fangio – the local hero who dominated Formula 1 motor racing in the 1950s – but for the moment football occupies pole position in the national consciousness, and the capital city is where it all happens. To see Diego Maradona's old team, Boca Juniors, head down to their stadium for cheap tickets. Since 2002, their ground has officially been called Estadio Alberto J Armando, but it will forever be known as the 'Biscuit Tin' – La Bombonera (*Brandsen 805, Boca. www.bocajuniors.com.ar*). For those who would rather experience matchday as part of a large escorted group, try Go Football (*Tel: (011) 4816 2681. www.gofootball.com.ar*). Their expensive packages to a variety of stadiums in

'Catch and release' is the norm

Buenos Aires offer poor value, but for end-of-season clashes, derby games or short-notice tickets, this is often the only option.

Golf

There are a number of excellent courses in the affluent suburbs of Buenos Aires, and in the beach resorts to the south of the capital. Players can swing away on the shores of Lago Nahuel Huapi, in sight of the historic Hotel Llao Llao, or play at the ends of the earth in Ushuaia, Tierra del Fuego. Patagonia Golf (*www.patagoniagolf.com*) has a good list of courses throughout the country.

Argentina's polo players are the best in the world

Horse riding

So at home are locals on the back of a horse, that polo is the national sport. Equestrian expeditions seem the obvious choice in Argentina, whether it's swinging in a gaucho saddle across the pampas, or you and your mount crossing the Andes on an epic one-week trip into Chile. Horse-riding opportunities have been identified throughout the destination pages.

Polo

Although the British ranchers brought polo over at the end of the last century, Argentineans are the world's best players, with the Heguy family very much at the top of the game. Historically, locals honed their skills in the ranches throughout the country, where today visitors can have a go at trying to ride a horse at full pelt while hitting a ball with a long mallet. The

main season runs from October to December, with the annual Polo Championship held in late November and early December at Campo Argentina de Polo in Palermo, Buenos Aires. This is the highlight of the polo calendar and tickets are almost impossible to get hold of. If you really want to attend, your best bet may be through a stay at a luxury estancia specialising in polo (*see pp163 & 172*), where some of the country's finest trainers of the sport and competitors are often to be found.

Skiing and snowboarding

For winter sports, South America is not the first place that springs to mind, but there are some very good slopes for both skiing and snowboarding in Argentina. Admittedly, snowfall can be unreliable, and technology – particularly in the smaller resorts – may be somewhat 'last-century', but the big advantage is that powder buffs from the northern hemisphere can take to the piste at a time (mid-June to mid-October) when resorts in Europe and the US have long since packed up for the year.

Spas

For those who take their activities lying down, spas in Argentina offer horizontal bliss in all forms. The native Mapuches and Tehuelches first used the natural healing hot springs, which today have been replaced by state-of-the-art Jacuzzis, saunas and steam rooms at boutique hotels and luxury estancias up and down the country. In Buenos Aires, day spas have become very popular. These are similar to what can be found in Europe and the US, but look out for local variations such as bathing in Cabernet Sauvignon in the wine region of Mendoza or getting smothered in Bariloche chocolate in the Lake District. Watch out for hotels that claim to be 'spas' but may have little more than a tiny and poorly maintained sauna.

Trekking

The scenic lakes around Bariloche and Torres del Paine, across the border in Chile, are particularly popular trekking spots that regularly keep walkers occupied for up to a week. But hikers can indulge their passion from the north to the south of the country and pretty much anywhere else in between. They can trek across the multicoloured desert of Quebrada de Humahuaca in the northeast, through the thick forests of Tierra del Fuego at the southern tip of the country, or over the pretty rolling slopes of the Central Sierras.

Take time out from hiking and horse riding and relax with a soothing massage

Children

The wide open spaces of the countryside, along with the welcoming attitude of Argentineans, make travelling with children largely a pleasure. Hotels, restaurants and tour companies provide for smaller travellers and often offer discounts for families. Do bear in mind, though, that distances are huge and many aspects, not least the language, will be foreign – difficult enough for adults but more so for children.

Wild child

Across Argentina, estancias are real-life theme parks where children can play at being cowboys, ride in historic *sulkies* (horse-drawn carriages), go fishing and enjoy encounters with farm animals. The thunderous roar of the spectacular Iguazú Falls and a close encounter with its 'Devil's Throat' will silence spectators of all ages. On the beaches of Península Valdés, meet sea lions, elephant seals and knee-high Magellenic penguins; offshore, keep an eye out for dolphins and great whales.

Thrilling rides

Take a boat trip to another country; Colonia in Uruguay with its pretty streets, beach and lighthouse is just a ferry ride away from Buenos Aires. Explore the turquoise waters of the Lake District on a catamaran, and make a unique 'mini trek' on the spectacular glacier of Perito Moreno (over 10s only). In Tierra del Fuego, take a dog-sledge ride through snowy valleys and step aboard the *Tren del fin del Mundo* (Train at the End of the World). Some lucky children will get the chance to make the trip of a lifetime to the icy landscape of Antarctica.

Fun food

Most restaurants offer the accepted favourites like pizza and pasta, and

Facepainting at La Bombonera (*see p145*)

many have a special children's menu. Most kids will love *licuados* (milk shakes) – usually with milk, but also with water – as well as *panchos* (hot dogs), desserts made from *dulce de leche* (caramelised condensed milk) and *helados* (ice cream). A real novelty will be the *submarino*; available in many cafés, this is a glass of hot milk served with a chocolate bar for dunking. (*See also* Food and Drink, *p136*.)

Playing in the park

All of Argentina's cities have green spaces and playgrounds that make a pleasant change from sightseeing. Hire bicycles or roller skates in Palermo Woods, where there is also a lake with boats for hire; there is even a planetarium with special shows for children. On the edge of the capital, Parque de la Costa (*www.parquedelacosta.com.ar*) is an enormous amusement fair with all the usual rides and a water park as well. In Córdoba, El Parque Sarmiento features a swimming pool, gardens and a zoo – enough entertainment for a full day.

A little learning

In the capital's Abasto shopping centre, the Museo de los Niños Abasto (*Av. Corrientes 3247, Abasto. www.museoabasto.org.ar, Spanish only*) is home to a scaled-down city where three- to twelve-year-olds can become anything from a crane driver to a TV presenter. The Prisoners' Museum in Ushuaia (*see p69*) is an atmospheric insight into the life of captives at the end of the earth a century ago. Also here is the Museo del Fin del Mundo with its stuffed birds and animals. Children will see a lot of great things in this country, but might also see six-year-olds collecting rubbish on the streets. Sponsoring a child whose parents are not there for them is a great way to teach your young ones that they can make a difference (*www.soschildrensvillages.org.uk*).

Children are welcome at the planetarium in Palermo's park

Children

Essentials

Arriving

Approximate flight time to Buenos Aires is 13 hours from London, 14 from New York, 16 from Los Angeles and 8½ from Miami. Most visitors fly into the capital's Ministro Pistarini International Airport (Ezeiza).

Customs

The following items are exempt from duty upon entrance to Argentina: 2 litres of alcohol (3½ pints), 400 cigarettes (20 packs) and 50 cigars.

Departing

From the centre of Buenos Aires, the international airport is around a 40-

Postcards home may take some time

minute drive. Expect to pay departure tax of around US$25, cash only in pesos or US dollars.

Electricity

Domestic power supply is 220V AC, 60Hz. Two different plug arrangements are in use: twin-round, and v-shaped twin with earth. Travellers should bring a world travel adapter.

Internet and email

Internet cafés can be found in all the main tourist areas. National parks and remote estancias are often cut off from all forms of communication, including email. WiFi is increasingly available in business and luxury hotels.

Money

Locals joke that tax-dodging is a national sport here. Even large hotels, restaurants and travel agencies will often only accept payment in cash. An increasingly common, but legal, phenomenon is for hotels and airlines to charge international visitors up to three times more than nationals. If prices are quoted in US dollars, it is an indication that there may be a two-tier system. Peso and dollar prices are often both preceded by '$', so be careful.

With ATMs, connections are often down and they frequently run out of money. The limit for each transaction can be as low as 400 pesos, which

The May Pyramid in Plaza de Mayo, Buenos Aires, commemorates the 1810 revolution

doesn't last long when even large hotels don't accept credit cards.

Opening hours

Many shops open long hours – often until 7 or 8pm – but close for a long lunch. Opening hours are unpredictable and changeable.

Passports and visas

Tourists from the United Kingdom, USA, Canada, Australia, New Zealand and South Africa do not require a visa to enter Argentina. Visitors from all other countries should check with their embassy. Anyone entering the country must have a passport valid for at least six months.

Pharmacies

Common medicines like antibiotics can be bought in *farmacias* (chemists/drug stores) quite cheaply and easily. Pharmacists are generally helpful with

Argentineans love to read

regard to minor ailments. Pharmacies in cities open 24 hours, and Farmacity is a chain that delivers.

Post and phone

Post is slow – it can easily take several weeks for a postcard or letter to arrive back home.

The cheapest way to make either a national or international phone call is from a payphone with a calling card bought in kiosks or newsagents.

When dialling Argentina from overseas, use your country's international access code followed by Argentina's country code (54), followed by the regional code (see above for examples) without the first zero, followed by the telephone number.

REGIONAL TELEPHONE CODES

02944	Bariloche
011	Buenos Aires
0351	Córdoba
02902	Calafate
0261	Mendoza
0387	Salta
02972	San Martín de los Andes
02901	Ushuaia

The majority of public phones accept tokens called *fichas* or *cospeles*, available from kiosks.

Public holidays

1 January – New Year's Day
March/April – Easter, Good Friday*
2 April – Veterans' Day (a tribute to the fallen in the Falklands War)

Look for shops with the 'Global Refund' sign to save on IVA tax

1 May – Labour Day
25 May – Anniversary of the first independent Argentine government
10 June – National Sovereignty Day
20 June – National Flag Day
9 July – National Independence Day
17 August – Anniversary of the death of General José de San Martín in 1850
12 October – Race Recognition Day
8 December – Immaculate Conception Day
25 December – Christmas Day

*The whole of Easter's Semana Santa (Holy Week) is a busy holiday time, with many people travelling.

Suggested reading

Crying with Cockroaches: Argentina to New York with Two Horses by Marianne Du Toit (2006). A heartfelt account of an emotional and inspiring journey. Despite the implicit animal rights message, this is not an earnest read.

At Home with the Patagonians: A Year's Wanderings over Untrodden Ground from the Straits of Magellan to the Río Negro by George Chaworth Musters (2005). A touching and considered account of a retired British general's experience of living and travelling with the Teheulche Indians in 1870.

Estancias (Palacios Criollos de Argentina) by Carolina and Aldo Sessa (2004). This spectacular photographic book does not come cheap but makes a fine and fascinating addition to any coffee table. English translation available.

The Real Odessa: How Peron Brought the Nazi War Criminals to Argentina by Uki Goni (2003). Scrupulous research has broken through the wall of silence to show how the Vatican and the President of Argentina sickeningly gave some of the last century's greatest war criminals an escape route out of Europe.

A Short History of the Argentinians by Félix Luna (2005). Although this condensed survey only begins with the Spanish occupation, it is a wonderful, thoughtful introduction to the country and its history.

A State of Fear: Memories of Argentina's Nightmare by Andrew Graham-Yooll (1986). The ex news editor of the liberal newspaper *The Buenos Aires Herald* gives a chilling insight into the kidnappings, tortures and murders that were everyday occurrences, particularly for journalists.

The Uttermost Part of the Earth: Indians of Tierra del Fuego by Lucas Bridges (1988). In 1874, the author became only the third white person ever to be born in Ushuaia, and grew up with Indians who are now essentially extinct. Bridges reveals his perceptive and adventurous spirit in this immensely enjoyable book.

Tax

Sales tax (IVA) is 21 per cent, added to hotel bills and retail purchases (*see p143*).

Time differences

Argentina is three hours behind

London, or four hours in British Summer Time (BST). Other time differences are listed below.

Auckland	+15 (+16)
Cape Town	+5
London	+3 (+4 BST)
Los Angeles	−5 (−4 PDT)
New York	−2 (−1 EDT)
Sydney	+13 (+14 EST)
Toronto	−2 (−1 EDT)

Toilets

Don't flush paper in the bowl as the sanitary system (other than those in international hotels) can't cope with it; instead put it in the bin provided. Note that the word for toilet is *baño* and bath is *bañero*.

Travellers with disabilities

Facilities for those with disabilities are poor in many regions of the country (*see p131*). However, some new hotels now provide at least one room suitable for visitors with a disability, and the waterfalls at Iguazú, for example, have been wheelchair accessible for some time.

Websites

www.travelsur.net A wealth of information from Erna Rosenfeld's highly recommended travel agency, TravelSur. Online booking service for hotels, flights and car hire, 'travel tools' and a destination guide.

www.parquesnacionales.gov.ar Although this fussy site can only be used with Internet Explorer, the contact details,

suggestions for walks, visuals and history are all useful.

http://interpatagonia.com Another informative site from a travel agency. As well as destination information, it has some nice touches, like recipes from local chefs.

www.welcomeargentina.com A new online guide covering the whole country, by the InterPatagonia people.

Don't forget to change your watch to Argentine time!

Language

Argentineans speak Spanish, which they call *Castellano*, with a distinct Italian accent, saying 'cho' instead of 'yo', for example. There are also some important differences in vocabulary, such as *vos* instead of *tú* – the plural of which is *ustedes* not *vosostros*. An 's' at the end of a word is rarely sounded. *Lunfardo* is a rich Buenos Aires slang that few tourists will get to grips with on a short trip.

It really is worth trying to speak at least a little Spanish in Argentina. Most Argentineans are incredibly patient, will listen to your bad Spanish without correcting it and take care to speak slowly so that you can understand them.

Many children are bilingual, learning English in school and speaking Spanish in the home. Most adults know at least some English, although they may lack confidence and be reluctant to speak it.

BASIC WORDS AND PHRASES
General Vocabulary

English	Spanish (pronunciation)
yes	*sí* (see)
no	*no* (no)
please	*por favor* (por faVOR)
thank you (very much)	*(muchas) gracias* ((MOOcaah) GRAseeya)
you're welcome	*de nada* (de NAda)
hello	*hola* (ola)
goodbye	*adiós* (adeeYO)
good morning/day	*buenas días* (BWEna DEEya)
good afternoon/evening	*buenas tardes* (BWEna TARde)
good evening (after dark)	*buenas noches* (BWEna NOche)
excuse me (to get attention)	*disculpe* (desKOOLpay)
excuse me (to apologise)	*perdón* (perDON)
sorry	*lo siento* (lo seeYENtoe)
help!	*!socorro!* (SOHcohroe)
today	*hoy* (oy)
tomorrow	*mañana* (manYAna)

English	Spanish (pronunciation)
yesterday	*ayer* (ayYER)
where?	*¿dónde?* (donday)
when?	*¿cuándo?* (KWANdo)
why?	*¿for qué?* (porKAY)
how?	*¿cómo?* (como)

Useful words and phrases

how much is it?	*¿cuánto es?* (KWANtoe e)
expensive	*caro/a* (KARo/a)
I don't understand	*no entiendo* (no enteeYENdoe)
do you speak English?	*habla usted inglés?* (ablah OOsted eenGLE)
my name is…	*me llamo…* (meh YAmoh..)

Toilet talk

plug	*tapón*
bath	*bañero*
toilet	*baño*

www.bbc.co.uk/languages/spanish/quickfix allows you to click on one of the basic words and hear it being spoken.

www.instaspanish.com is a more complete resource with structured MP3s, forums and downloadable printouts.

With just the basics, it is easy to strike up a friendship

Emergencies

Emergency numbers
Police   101
Fire   100
Medical 107

Police and the tourist police
The Tourist Police is a special unit of the Federal Police set up to respond to tourists 24 hours a day, seven days a week, with English-speaking assistance. There is an office in Buenos Aires (*Avenida Corrientes 436. Tel: (11) 4346 5770*) as well as a nationwide toll-free number (*Tel: 0800 999 0500*).

Health care
Even though Argentina's public health service gives free medical assistance to everyone, take out health insurance before travelling. Look for cheap deals on the internet, but carefully check what is covered, particularly if you are planning adventure activities. Annual cover costs little more than single-trip policies and is well worth investigating.

Most visitors to Argentina will not require vaccinations, but if staying for longer than six months, or travelling extensively in jungle areas such as Missiones, consult a doctor at least two months in advance.

Be wary of the sun on the pampas and in desert areas like Salta – wear high-factor sun cream, sunglasses and a light-coloured hat. Bacterial diarrhoea, if it strikes, will usually clear up within a week, but to avoid severe dehydration consume plenty of electrolytic drinks – you can get dissolvable powders in almost every pharmacy. Outside of obviously well-set up restaurants and hotels, you are advised to drink bottled rather than tap water.

Safety and crime
Traffic probably presents the greatest danger to visitors, both passengers and pedestrians; take particular care when crossing the road, as many drivers ignore red lights, especially when turning right.

Petty crime
The vast majority of foreign visitors experience no problems in Argentina, but all should avoid displaying valuables or carrying large amounts of cash. Petty crime does occur, particularly in Buenos Aires. Only carry what is necessary, stay alert and avoid unlit or unpopulated areas, especially if alone at night. If confronted, comply with a criminal's requests to hand over money or possessions, as they may turn violent.

Money scams
Con artists always seem to have a latest trick, so it is impossible for anyone, including guidebook writers, to keep up. Currently, the authorities suggest noting the last two digits of large banknote serial numbers to prevent

note switching. In taxis, and even in hotels, always agree any price beforehand and keep your wits about you. A common ruse is to take your note and hand back change for a smaller one; before you hand over a large banknote for a small purchase, show your note first and ask whether they have change (*¿Tienes cambio?*).

Drugs

Argentina lies on a drug-smuggling route to the USA, and penalties for possession of even small amounts of illegal drugs are severe. If you are offered drugs, be very careful. You could potentially be walking into a police trap, and be facing a stiff prison sentence.

Embassies and consulates

If you get into trouble with the police, have an accident, lose your passport, or become a victim of crime, you might need to contact your embassy or consulate, so check you have their details before your visit. If you're planning to stay a few months it's also a good idea to register with them.

Australian Embassy

Villanueva 1400, Buenos Aires. Tel: (011) 4779 3500. www.argentina.embassy.gov.au

British Embassy

Dr Luis Agote 2412, Buenos Aires, Tel: (011) 4808 2200. www.britishembassy.gov.uk

Canadian Embassy

Tagle 2828, Buenos Aires. Tel: (011) 4808 1000. http://geo.international.gc.ca

New Zealand Consulate

Carlos Pellegrini 1427, 5th Floor, Buenos Aires. Tel: (011) 4328 0747. www.nzembassy.com

South African Embassy

Avenida Marcelo T de Alvear 590, 8th Floor, Buenos Aires. Tel: (011) 4317 2900. www.embajadasudafrica.org.ar

US Embassy

Av. Colombia 4300, Buenos Aires. Tel: (011) 5777 4533. http://argentina.usembassy.gov

Many of the aforementioned countries also have consulates in other major cities. See their websites for more details. Finally, it's always a good idea to check your government's advice before you travel.

In La Boca, stick to the tourist areas

Directory

Accommodation price guide

★	Up to 150 pesos
★★	150–300 pesos
★★★	300–450 pesos
★★★★	Over 450 pesos

A scale of 1–4 stars has been used as a price guide, with 1 star indicating the cheapest option and 4 stars the most expensive. Price bands are based on the average cost of a double room. Often, an additional bed can be added to a room for a fraction of the total. Credit cards are widely accepted in the cities, but not always in remote villages or at estancias in the middle of the countryside. If you are planning to pay with a card, check it is accepted at the time of booking. Although significant fluctuations in exchange rates seem to be a thing of the past, prices, particularly for accommodation, are rarely static, so check the latest information and then budget accordingly. Some hotels use an average exchange rate to make their charges, which rarely benefit the customer. Estancias offer excellent value for money, usually providing excellent accommodation, four meals a day with drinks and even activities such as horse riding in their room rate.

Eating out price guide

★	Up to 30 pesos
★★	30–60 pesos
★★★	60–120 pesos
★★★★	Over 120 pesos

The star system below is based on the average price of a meal for one person without drinks or tips. Eating out is an important social event for Argentineans, whatever their financial situation. Although most establishments are incredibly good value for overseas visitors, in Buenos Aires especially and also in gastronomic enclaves such as Mendoza, there are no shortage of world-class restaurants, with prices to match.

Addresses may be given without a street number, such as 'Morales esq. Gamarra'. In such cases 'esq' is short for *esquina* (corner), so head to the first street where the second street crosses it.

BUENOS AIRES
In the City
ACCOMMODATION
La Otra Orilla ★★
Perhaps the best budget option in Palermo. A mother and daughter have opened the doors of their charming family home to tourists. There is a range of rooms, but book ahead as the prices make this a popular choice.
Julián Álvarez 1779, Palermo.

Tel: (011) 4867 4070.
www.otraorilla.com.ar
Casa de 1890 ★★★
Very comfortable B&B,
with just three rooms
(two with Jacuzzis) in a
large 19th-century house
in San Telmo. Prides
itself on its art, history
and hospitality, as well as
its fine bed linen.
Humberto Primo 843.
Tel: (011) 4300 1890.
www.buenosaires1890byb.
com.ar
Buenos Aires
Rent ★★–★★★★
Even for short stays,
this firm offers some
of the best-value
accommodation in the
capital. Apartments in
Palermo and around the
city – from studios to
four bedrooms – can be
viewed online. Paula, the
friendly and efficient
owner, speaks perfect
English and also offers a
concierge service.
Tel: (011) 4827 9293.
www.buenosairesrent.com
Art Hotel ★★★
This boutique hotel is
often full, so book ahead.
Argentinean works of art
decorate the walls, and
all the rooms, including a
living room and bar, are

simple, yet stylish. The
owner and staff are
delightful and can
arrange interesting tours.
Azcuenaga 1268, Palermo.
Tel: (011) 4821 4744.
www.arthotel.com.ar
Alvear Palace Hotel ★★★★
This hotel is wonderfully
traditional, with service
to match. Recently made
an historic landmark, the
sumptuous bar is open to
the public and Sunday
brunch in the Orangery
is a local institution
(*noon–4pm, smart-casual
dress required*). A new
health club opened in
2007.
Av. Alvear 1891, Retiro.
Tel: (011) 4808 2100.
www.alvearpalace.com

EATING OUT
Aconcagua ★
A basic, clean, air-
conditioned café/bar
that is a welcome retreat
from the throngs of
tourists on the main
drag. Large menu
including omelettes,
bargain set meals, great
salads and fresh orange
juice; there is also space
at the bar to enjoy a
beer and some olives
with the locals.

Estados Unidos 506 esq.
Bolívar. San Telmo.
Jardín Japonés ★★
This air-conditioned
restaurant overlooking
the carp-filled lake of the
Japanese Garden is a real
oasis in the city. Enjoy
sushi, noodles or melt-
in-your-mouth tempura
washed down with sake
or an 'Asahi' beer. An
entrance fee is payable
for the garden so take
in the grounds and
maybe an exhibition
after your meal.
Av. Casares y Figueroa
Alcorta, Palermo.
Tel: (011) 4804 9141.
www.jardinjapones.com.ar
Spell Café ★★
During the day, stop
for coffee or enjoy a
lunch of local and
ethnic dishes between
shopping in the local
boutiques. This spacious,
friendly venue on
several floors has
internet access and
transforms into a
popular nightspot late
in the evening.
Malabia 1738, Palermo.
Tel: (011) 4832 3389.
El Trapiche ★★★
Rounded, jolly waiters
provide a leisurely service

at this local institution. The stone floors, huge fans and linen tablecloths provide a cool backdrop for customers tucking into perfectly cooked meat, paella and the occasional fish dish.
Paraguay 5099, Palermo. Tel: (011) 4772 7343.

La Bourgogne ★★★★
Decadent French cuisine, the best in the whole country, in a luxurious and historic setting.
Av. Alvear 1891, Retiro. Tel: (011) 4805 3857. www.alvearpalace.com

Teresita ★★★★
Ideally, complete a one-day cookery class and then tuck into your own creations. Or, enjoy a three-course Latin American meal and fine wine for lunch or dinner, with three menus to choose from. A half-hour journey from the city centre.
Spiro 456, Adrogue. Tel: (011) 4293 5992. www.try2cook.com

ENTERTAINMENT
Café Tortoni
Tango shows twice a night, but this BA institution is worth a

daytime visit too, for cocktails or tea.
Av. de Mayo 825, Central BA. Tel: (011) 4342 4328.

El Viejo Almacén
Dinner and dance shows in this historic house of tango.
Avenida Independencia y Balcarce, San Telmo. Tel: (011) 4307 6689. www.viejoalmacen.com

Escuela Argentina de Tango
Various cultural centres, as well as schools, stage tango events and offer group and individual classes. This is one of the best.
Galerías Pacífico, Centro Cultural Borges, Viamonte esq. San Martín. Tel: (011) 4312 4990. www.eatango.org

Mott
This stylish, airy, loft-like bar is straight out of SoHo, New York. Sip one of the delicious cocktails, such as a sake and grape *caipirinha*, while lounging on the velvet day beds. The food sounds tempting, but tends to disappoint.
El Salvador 4685, Palermo. Tel: (011) 4833 4306.

Opera Bay
Looks like Sydney's opera house, but is actually a bar and nightclub, with great views of the docks. Wednesdays are fun, when locals party after work. Mostly tourists at the weekend.
Cecilia Grierson 225, Puerto Madero. Tel: (15) 5247 0565. www.operabay.com

Talk time
Locals get together in local cafés to discuss the topics of the day and practise their English. Tourists are positively welcomed. The *Buenos Aires Herald* lists conversation groups. (*www.talktime.com.ar*)

SPORT AND LEISURE
Asociación Argentina de Polo
Polo matches take place in Buenos Aires from September to mid-November, but the undisputed highlight of the polo calendar is the annual *Campeonato Argentino Abierto* (Argentine Open Polo Championship) in Palermo. The association can provide details of

polo matches and
activities throughout
Argentina.
*Tel: (011) 4777 6444.
Arévalo 3065.
www.aapolo.com in
Spanish only.*

**Panda Bike Hire and
Tours**
Bike hire from one hour
to a week (passport
required). Maps and
MP3 downloads with full
circuits and highlights
are available. Also, full-
day guided tours though
woods and a nature
reserve.
*Ruggieri 2778, Palermo.
Tel: (011) 4804 6654.
www.pandabikeandtours.
com*

The Pampas
ACCOMMODATION
Antigua Casona ★★
Historic house offering
bed and breakfast. Three
bedrooms, a beautiful
museum-like kitchen,
and an exquisite
courtyard, all
tastefully restored
and decorated by an
antique dealer.
*Segundo Sombra 495,
San Antonio de Areco.
Tel: (02326) 456 600.
www.antiguacasona.com*

**Estancia Los Dos
Hermanos ★★**
Rooms or whole cabins
for rent, a pool and
horse-riding trips for all
the family, in a relaxed
rustic setting (*see p41*).
*Ruta 193. Km 10.5,
Escalada, Zárate.
Tel: (011) 4765 4320.
www.estancialosdos
hermanos.com*

Paradores Draghi ★★★
Small, formal hotel with
a garden and a museum.
*Lavalle 387, San Antonio
de Areco.
Tel: (02326) 455 583.
www.sanantoniodeareco.
com/turismo*

Estancia El Rocio ★★★★
The owner, Patrice, is
justly proud of this
luxurious estancia.
Excellent food, fishing,
polo, horse and *sulky*
rides and a swimming
pool. No young children
allowed, however.
*(See p41.)
Ruta 3, Km 102.5,
San Miguel del Monte.
Tel: (02271) 420 488.
www.estanciaelrocio.com*

EATING OUT
**Almacén de Ramos
Generales ★★★**
This popular restaurant

in a 150-year-old house
filled with antiques is big
on atmosphere and
service. *Parrillas* (grills)
and pastas, mussels
and trout are all on
the menu.
*Zapiola 143, San
Antonio de Areco.
Tel: (02326) 456 376.
www.ramosgeneralesareco.
com.ar*

Iguazú and around
ACCOMMODATION
**Tropical das
Cataratas ★★★★**
On the Brazilian side,
this luxurious, pricey
hotel is perched right on
the edge of the famous
falls.
*BR 469 km28, Parque
Nacional do Iguaçu.
Tel: +55 (45) 3521 7000.
www.tropicalhotel.com.br*

**Estancia Santa Cecilia
★★★★**
A lovely working cattle
ranch close to the Jesuit
ruins of Misiones. Relax
on the veranda and in
the pool, or horse ride
with the gauchos and
cattle ranchers. All
activities and full board
included.
*Km 1366, Ruta Nacional
12, 30km (18¹/₂ miles)*

from Posadas.
Tel: (03752) 493 018.
www.santacecilia.com.ar

Sheraton Internacional Iguazú Resort ★★★★
The building is a real blot on the landscape, but it is the only hotel within the national park, allowing access away from the crowds. It costs considerably more for a room with a view of the Falls.
Parque Nacional Iguazú.
Tel: (03757) 491 800.
www.sheraton.com

Yacutinga Lodge ★★★★
An award-winning eco-lodge and research station with separate accommodation in its own private reserve. Price includes full board, transfer from the airport by jeep and boat, and walking and wildlife excursions in the rainforest.
Upper Iguazú River, 60km (37 miles) from the Falls.
No phone.
www.yacutinga.com

EATING OUT
The Sheraton and Cataracts hotels both have decent restaurants. Food in Puerto Iguazú,

the nearest town, is mediocre at best and involves a taxi ride. Accommodation at Estancia Santa Cecilia and Yacutinga Lodge includes all meals.

CENTRAL AND SOUTHERN PATAGONIA

ACCOMMODATION

Cabañas Nueva León ★
Lodgings in Puerto Madryn are generally overpriced and of a poor standard. Visitors should consider these great value self-catering cottages, offered by Susana Piacenza.
Namuncura 761,
Puerto Madryn.
Tel: (02965) 472 635.
www.nuevaleon.com.ar

Hotel Bahia ★–★★
Basic but clean lodgings in this small Atlantic port.
Av. San Martín 1075,
Puerto San Julián.
Tel: (02962) 453 144.
www.hotelbahiasanjulian.com.ar

El Galpón del Glaciar ★★
This remote hostel, halfway between El Calafate and the Perito Moreno glacier, is

popular with hikers. Live demonstrations of sheep shearing draw day trippers.
Km 22 Ruta 11, near
El Calafate.
Tel: (02902) 491 793.
www.estanciaalice.com.ar

Design Suites El Calafate ★★★★
A dramatic setting on the hills above Calafate with great views of the lake. Fine, friendly service, comfortable rooms, a great pool and a spa. Few restaurants in the city have decent views of the lake. The restaurant in Design Suites does, with above-average food on offer, too. Avoid the group's Bariloche hotel, which is awful.
Calle 94, No. 190,
Playa Lago Argentino,
El Calafate.
Tel: (02902) 494 525.
www.designsuites.com

Hostería Los Notros ★★★★
The only option for those who want to sleep within sight and sound of the famous Moreno glacier is this ultra-expensive hotel.
Parque Nacional
Los Glaciares.

Tel: (011) 4814 3934.
www.losnotros.com
Remota ★★★★
The excellent modern
design of this hotel
blends perfectly with the
environment. It has a full
range of excursions into
the nearby Torres del
Paine national park,
sauna and pool and is
popular with tour
groups.
Puerto Natales, Chile.
Tel: +56 (61) 414 040.
www.remota.cl
Hotel Salto Chico ★★★★
Excursions, a spa and all-
inclusive food and wine.
Excursions into Parque
Nacional Torres del Paine
with helpful, bilingual
guides. Minimum stay of
four nights.
Lago Pehoé, PN Torres del
Paine. Office: Américo
Vespucio Sur 80, Piso 5,
Santiago, Chile.
Tel: (+56) (2) 206 6060.
www.explora.com
Los Cerros ★★★★
This new, hulking hotel
is the most comfortable
place to stay in El
Chaltén. Although more
functional than
luxurious, anyone staying
here will be out all day
on hikes and the hotel

offers a full programme
of guided excursions.
Los Cerros, El Chaltén.
Tel: (02962) 493 182.
www.loscerrosdelchalten.
com

EATING OUT

Besides the options listed
below, try the hotels
above, where the
restaurants are among
the best in their
respective areas.
Ricks Café ★
Established barbecue
and pasta house,
popular with
backpackers.
Av. Libertador 1105,
El Calafate.
Tel: (02902) 492 148.
San Guchito ★
Good seafood at both
branches of this local
favourite.
Av. Brown (esq. Perlotti
and Av. 25 de Mayo) 245,
Puerto Madryn.
Cantina El Náutico ★★★
A well-estabished classic
in town, well known for
its seafood and very
popular, even with
celebrities. Don't miss
the cold seafood starter.
There is also a delivery
service.
Julio A Roca Av. 790,

Puerto Madryn.
Tel: (02965) 471 404.
www.cantinaelnautico.
com.ar
Ty Gwyn ★
This Welsh teahouse,
where the tablecloths are
gingham and the
waitresses wear Welsh
costumes, serves up
traditional cakes, scones
and sandwiches and
more.
9 de Julio 111, Gaiman.
Tel: (02965) 491 009.
www.cpatagonia.com/gai
man/ty-gwyn

ENTERTAINMENT
La Toldería
Busy hub of the frontier
town's nightlife scene –
the informal restaurant
is transformed into a
nightclub at around
11pm.
Av. Libertador 1177,
El Calafate.
Margarita Pub
Nightlife in Puerto
Madryn is decidedly low-
key, but this pub offers
live music, changing
events, decent cocktails
and bar food in a historic
building. There is a
second venue in Trelew
at Fontana 19.
Roque Saenz Peña 15,

Puerto Madryn.
Tel: (02965) 475 871.
www.margaritapub.com

Santino

A modern, yet cosy bar with cocktails and live music on Saturdays. The Italian owners have put their native cuisine, along with international offerings on the menu.
Av. Colón 657, Punta Arenas, Chile.
Tel: +56 (61) 5671 0882.
www.santino.cl

SPORT AND LEISURE

Aventura Andina

A friendly company offering a variety of glacier tours, including boat-based excursions and 4×4 trips. Deal direct with Hielo y Aventura (*Libertador 935.*
Tel: (02902) 492 205.
www.hieloyaventura.com)
if all you are after is a walk on the icy giant.
Av. Libertador 761,
El Calafate.
Tel: (02902) 492 112.
www.aventura-andina.
com.ar

Big Foot

Dramatic multi-day kayaking trips in the icy fjords of the Chilean national park.

Bories 206, Puerto Natales, Torres del Paine.
Tel: (+56) (61) 414 525.
www.indomitapatagonia.
com

Fitz Roy Expediciones

Experienced and safety-conscious guides run a number of mountain survival schools, together with a wide variety of trekking, climbing, horse riding and mountain-bike tours.
Lionel Terray 545,
El Chaltén.
Tel: (02962) 493 017.
www.fitzroyexpediciones.
com.ar

Whales Argentina

Captain Pinino runs one of the most respected whale-watching operations on the peninsula.
Primera Bajada,
Puerto Pirámides,
Península Valdés.
Tel: (02965) 495 015.
www.whalesargentina.
com.ar

TIERRA DEL FUEGO

ACCOMMODATION

El Camping Lago Roca ★

The only official campsite in the national park (there are several unofficial ones), right on

Lago Roca, in the forest. Clean facilities, with a café, food shop and campfire areas.
Parque Nacional Tierra del Fuego, 21km (13 miles) west of Ushuaia.
Tel: (02901) 433 313 / (02901) 15 608 930.

Galeazzi–Basily B&B ★–★★

A friendly, family home in the centre, with two twin rooms sharing a bathroom and three cabins with kitchenettes (sleeping four or eight people). One of the best budget choices in town, especially for families.
Gob. Valdez 323, Ushuaia.
Tel: (02901) 423 213.
www.avesdelsur.com.ar

Hostéria Tierra de Leyendas ★★★★

Elegantly designed with wonderful views over the Beagle Channel and just a short taxi ride out of town. The welcoming husband and wife team and excellent restaurant make this a much better choice than the disappointing and over-priced Las Hayas.
Calle sin nombre 2387,
Tierra de Leyendas,
Ushuaia. Tel: (02901)

443 565. *www.*
tierradeleyendas.com.ar

Eating out
Patagonia Mia ★★–★★★
At the entrance to the
national park, this
teashop and restaurant
specialises in local dishes.
Ruta Nacional, 3km,
Parque Nacional
Tierra del Fuego.
Tel: (02901) 422 907.
www.patagoniamia.com
Volver ★★★
Popular and historic
restaurant filled with
antiques and decorated
with old newspapers. The
signature dish is king
crab, but the wide menu
featuring all sorts of
seafood, as well as local
meat dishes, has enough
to keep everyone happy.
Av. Maipú 37, Ushuaia.
Tel: (02901) 423 977.
Kaupé ★★★★
The almost faultless
haute cuisine using local
produce regularly earns
this intimate restaurant
the title of 'best
restaurant in Argentina'.
The tasting menu,
including wine and
dessert, is good value and
highly recommended.
Roca 470, Ushuaia.

Tel: (02901) 422 704.
www.kaupe.com.ar

Entertainment
Club Naútico
This and the Lenon Pub,
also on the waterfront,
are the two most popular
drinking holes in the city.
Both have their fair share
of locals and stay open
until 6am, but Naútico
has dancing at weekends.
Maipú 1210, Ushuaia.
Tel: (02901) 421 024.

Sport and leisure
Cruceros Australis
Cruises on two luxury
vessels in the Magellan
Strait and the Beagle
Channel, as well as
three- or four-night
sailings to Punto
Arenas in Chile.
Carlos Pellegrini 989, Piso
6, Buenos Aires.
Tel: (011) 4325 8400.
www.australis.com
Victory Adventure
Expeditions
This company is sensitive
to both the environment
and the indigenous
history of the area. Based
in Chile but offers many
sailings from Ushuaia,
including kayaking,
Tierra del Fuego, the

Beagle Channel and
Antarctica.
Tel: (61) 62 10 10.
www.victory-cruises.com

THE LAKE DISTRICT
Accommodation
Los Bagueanos
Cablagatas ★
A couple of kilometres
from Peuma Hue, and
sharing the same lake
and mountain scenery,
is this rustic dorm-style
lodge and camp
ground, a good horse-
riding and hiking
base for travellers
on a budget.
Cabecera Sur del Lago
Gutiérrez. Tel: (02944)
(15) 554 362.
La Cheminée ★★
Homely hotel in the
Swiss alpine mould,
with better breakfasts
than its more expensive
competitors in the area.
Roca y Moreno, San
Martín de los Andes.
Tel: (02972) 427 617.
www.hosterialacheminee.
com.ar
Estancia Peuma Hue ★★★
Idyllic lakeside cabins,
log fires, fine wines
and food made with
love. Massage treatments,
wine tasting and a host

of outdoor activities for all age groups.

Cabecera Sur del Lago Gutiérrez, Km 25, Ruta 258. Tel: (02944) 15 501 030 / (011) 15 5101 1392. www.peuma-hue.com

Río Manso Lodge ★★★

Anglers who like a bit of luxury head to this riverside retreat in the Lake District.

Tel: (02944) 490 546. www.riomansolodge.com

Hostería Isla Victoria ★★★★

The island's only hotel is an exclusive and luxurious affair with a two-night minimum stay, but the fishing, hiking, birding and horse riding will more than keep you busy in the day, and at night there is fine food and the luxurious spa.

Isla Victoria, Parque Nacional Nahuel Huapi. Tel: (02944) 448 088. www.islavictoria.com

Hotel Tronador ★★★★

On the shore of Lago Mascardi, with its own dock and views of snow-capped mountains, this family-run hotel is as picturesque as they come. Fine homemade food and a good base for outdoor activities in this area.

Brazo Tronador, 60km (37 miles) from Bariloche. Tel: (02944) 441 062. www.hoteltronador.com

Villa Huinid ★★★★

Great for families, it has a children's play area and luxury cabins for up to eight people. For children over four years old, supervised activities include swimming and games in the pool, forest mini-treks, painting and a bedtime movie. Babysitting for toddlers. For adults, there is the pool, Jacuzzi, steam room and a range of spa treatments.

Av. Bustillo Km 2.6, Bariloche. Tel: (02944) 523 523. www.villahuinid.com.ar

EATING OUT

La Costa del Pueblo ★★

A traditional *parrilla* (grill house) with views over the lake.

Av. Costanera y Obei, San Martín de los Andes. Tel: (02972) 429 289.

Cassis ★★★

Fusion of European and Patagonian cuisine served in a great location overlooking Lago Gutiérrez.

Sobre el Peñón de Arelauquen Ruta 82, Lago Gutiérrez. Tel: (02944) 476 167. www.cassis-patagonia.com.ar. Open: lunch until 4pm, afternoon tea and dinner from 8pm. Reservations essential in peak season, credit cards not accepted.

SPORT AND LEISURE

Aukache

Full- and half-day trekking, kayaking, climbing and rappel/abseiling all around the Lake District.

Tel: (02944) 456 388 /

INSIDER TIP: THE MAIN DRAG

The hotels listed above offer some of the best dining opportunities in the Lake District. In Bariloche, give the dull main streets of San Martín and Moreno a miss when it comes to eating and drinking. At Trentis on the lake, locals feast on pizzas, piled high with fresh toppings, and friendly staff mix perfect cocktails 24 hours a day.

Rosas 435, Bariloche. Tel: (02944) 422 350.

(02944) 15 611 561.
www.aukache.com

Bike Way
Bike hire in Bariloche.
Sale and hire of hiking
and climbing equipment,
binoculars, GPS devices.
Delivery anywhere in or
around Bariloche.
Moreno 237, Bariloche.
Tel: (02944) 456 571.
www.bikeway.com.ar

Cau Cau
Large double-hulled
tourist boats (with
disabled access) make
whirlwind trips from
Puerto Pañuelo, stopping
at Isla Victoria (up to
3 hours; see p168), and
then the Bosque de los
Arrayanes forest
(50 minutes). Coach
transfers from Bariloche
are available but only
recommended if you
want to spend an hour
picking up guests from
other hotels.
Mitre 139, Bariloche.
Tel: (02944) 431 372. www.
islavictoriaarrayanes.com

Del Lago Turismo
Day trips across Lago
Mascardi, with hiking to
the glacier and waterfall
at Cerro Tronador.
Villegas 222, Bariloche.
Tel: (02944) 430 056.

Extremo Sur
Reliable group,
organising a variety of
rafting (Class II to IV)
and kayaking expeditions
on the Río Manso (see
p84) and southern lakes.
One-day and multi-day
trips are available, the
latter offering the chance
to camp in the middle of
Parque Nahuel Huapi.
Expect to get wet, but
safety standards are high.
Morales 765, Bariloche.
Tel: (02944) 427 301.
www.extremosur.com

Pura Vida Patagonia
Professional kayak
excursions on the lakes
and rivers – less
challenging than
Extremo Sur, these are
more sightseeing tours
by canoe, with the ability
to accommodate the
mobility-impaired in
robust two-person
kayaks. Guides speak
good English.
Tel: (02944) 448 793.
www.puravidapatagonia.
com.ar

MENDOZA AND WINE COUNTRY

ACCOMMODATION

Casa Glebinias ★ ★
Two rustic lodges with

kitchen and living area in
lovely grounds on the
edge of Mendoza city at
this relaxing, reasonably
priced spot, where the
helpful owners bring you
breakfast each morning.
Chacras de Coria.
Tel: (0261) 496 211.

Cavas Wine Lodge ★★★★
Set in 24ha (60 acres)
on the wine route
(see p94), this luxury
lodge is peaceful yet
very convenient for the
bodegas. Romantic, with
excellent service,
spacious, well-equipped
rooms and a spa.
Costaflores s/n, Alto
Agrelo.
Tel: (0261) 410 6927.
www.cavaswinelodge.com

Finca Adalgisa ★ ★ ★ ★
This lovely rural winery
12km (7½ miles) south
of Mendoza allows
visitors to combine
attractive lodging with
free wine tasting. The
pool, wine bar and
restaurant are definite
pluses.
Pueyrredón 2222, Chacras
de Coria.
Tel: (0261) 496 0713.
www.fincaadalgisa.com.ar

Valle de Uco Lodge ★★★★
An exclusive retreat

90km (56 miles) from Mendoza City, with vineyards, orchards and pool. Wonderful service, personalised wine and adventure tours even for non-residents, and a farmhouse that is particularly good for families.

Tabanera s/n, Colonia Las Rosas, Tunuyán.
Tel: (02622) 490 102 / 496 1888.
www.postalesdelplata.com

EATING OUT

Azafrán ★

Enjoy tapas such as crab with ginger, venison ravioli and wine tastings at this charming establishment. The delicatessen next door is not to be missed.

Av. Sarmiento 765, City of Mendoza.
Tel: (0261) 429 4200.
www.azafranalmacenes. com.ar

Marisquería Praga ★★

Spanish tapas and seafood dishes have a 50-year-old tradition in Mendoza, to which this restaurant in a 19th-century house pays homage.

Leonidas Aguirre 413,

City of Mendoza.
Tel: (0261) 425 9585.

Almacén del Sur ★★★

An elegant farmhouse restaurant and cottage factory 15km (9 miles) from Mendoza, open for lunch only (reservations essential).

Sanichelli 709, Coquimbito. Tel: (0261) 410 6597.
www.almacendelsur.com

1884 Francis Mallmann ★★★★

Considered by some to be Argentina's best restaurant. Exquisite cuisine using Patagonian ingredients, French cooking methods and a clay oven. It is part of the Bodega Escorihuela, so why not combine lunch with a tour? Reservations essential.

Belgrano 1188, Godoy Cruz.
Tel: (0261) 424 2698.
www.escorihuela.com.ar

ENTERTAINMENT

Café del Tiempo

An atmospheric, intimate watering hole straight out of BA's San Telmo that also serves food and puts on live shows. Its sister operation is Frida, a lively

pub/restaurant at no. 935 on the same street.

Balcarce 901, Salta.
Tel: (0387) 432 0771.
www.cafedeltiempo.com

El Boliche Balderrama

Authentic folkloric shows combining music, poetry and dance are put on nightly at this intimate, family-run venue with a long history. Go for dinner too, or just dessert.

San Martín 1126, Salta.
Tel: (0387) 421 1542.
www.boliche-balderrama.com.ar

Lupulo

A cavernous, modern microbrewery that gets lively later in the evening. Good snacks and bar meals also available. The whole street is lined with bars, some with live music.

Av. Arístides Villanueva 471, City of Mendoza.
Tel: (0261) 427 0270.
www.ellupulo.com.ar

Park Hyatt

Admittedly not big on local atmosphere, this large international hotel does deliver on comfort and variety. Uvas is a cocktail and wine bar with live music most nights and weekly wine tastings, and there is even a casino.

Chile 1124, City of Mendoza. Tel: (0261) 441 1234. www. mendoza.park.hyatt.com

SPORT AND LEISURE
Ríos Andinos
A whole range of adventure activities in the countryside around Mendoza, including rafting, kayaking and horse riding.
Sarmiento 721, City of Mendoza.
Tel: (0261) 429 5030.
www.riosandinos.com

Trekking Travel
Professional yet friendly adventure tour company specialising in trekking (half-day to Aconcagua ascent) and riding (half-day to crossing the Andes) tours; also rock climbing, rafting and mountain biking.
Adolfo Calle 4171, Guaymallén. Tel: (0261) 421 0450. www.trekking-travel.com.ar

CÓRDOBA AND THE CENTRAL SIERRAS
ACCOMMODATION
Hotel Victoria ★★
This elegant, English-

style building dates from 1929. Enjoy a gin and tonic by the pool or on the terrace overlooking the golf course, a civilised breakfast until 11.30am and faultless, Mediterranean-style food. No children under 12 allowed.
Posadas 555, La Cumbre. Tel: (03548) 451 412. www.hotelvictoria.com.ar

The King David Hotel ★★
A contemporary offering with mini apartments at great prices, small rooftop pool and business centre. Vague service, but bargain set menus.
Av. General Paz 386, City of Córdoba.
Tel: (0351) 570 3528.
www.kingdavid.com.ar

El Colibri ★★★★
This exclusive 'rural palace' is a member of Relais and Chateaux. Its enormous grounds include a pool, polo fields, a spa and wine cellar. There are plenty of activities, including many that will appeal to children, such as fishing and go-karting.
Camino a Santa Catalina Km7, Santa Catalina.

Tel: (03525) 465 888.
www.estanciaelcolibri.com

Estancia La Paz ★★★★
This estancia's enormous lake can be seen from the road. It offers riding and relaxation as well as day trips.
E66, 4km (2¹/₂ miles) before Ascochinga.
Tel: (03525) 492 073/156 476 16.
www.estancialapaz.com

EATING OUT
La Nieta e La Pancha ★★
Friendly place serving excellent, locally sourced food and delicious sauces in an unpretentious but charming restaurant, with very reasonable prices.
Belgrano 783, City of Córdoba.
Tel: (0351) 424 7916.

La Casona del Toboso ★★★
Impeccable food and service are lapped up by the locals who flock to this 'house' with pretty garden. It is a traditional *parrilla* and pasta restaurant with a wide-ranging menu.
Belgrano 349, La Cumbre. Tel: (03548) 451 436.

ENTERTAINMENT

El Arrabal

Dinner and tango shows from Thursday to Saturday are a local institution; also tango classes. Reservations essential.
Belgrano 899, City of Córdoba.
Tel: (0351) 460 2990.

SPORT AND LEISURE

Itati

Adventure tours, trekking and paragliding, golf in the countryside around Córdoba and even further afield.
27 de Abril 220, City of Córdoba. Tel: (0351) 422 5020. www.itati.com.ar (Spanish only).

SALTA AND SURROUNDS

ACCOMMODATION

El Lagar ★★★

The memory of this hotel, which deliberately doesn't advertise or have a website, will stay with you long after your trip. Enormous rooms in a colonial mansion that is more like a home than a hotel, with the owner always on hand. Ideally located close to the action but in a quiet street.
20 de Febrero 875, City of Salta. Tel: (0387) 431 9439. ellagar@arnet.com.ar

Estancia El Bordo de Las Lanzas ★★★★

Traditional hospitality with a full programme of activities as well as delicious cuisine at this 400-year-old colonial estancia in the foothills of the Andes.
Rivadavia, El Bordo, Av. General Guemes, 25km (15½ miles) from Jujuy. Tel: (0387) 490 3070. www. turismoelbordo.com.ar

The House of Jasmines ★★★★

Actor Robert Duvall owns this exquisite, 100-year-old hacienda surrounded by 121½ha (300 acres) of land. Romantic and relaxing, activities and meals are not included in the price.
Ruta 51, Km 11, La Merced Chica, 20km (12½ miles) from Salta. Tel: (0387) 497 2002. www.houseofjasmines.com

EATING OUT

El Solar del Convento ★★

Perhaps the city's best restaurant, but very reasonably priced.

Authentic cuisine including lots of barbecued meat in a rustic, elegant setting.
Caseros 444, Salta. Tel: (0387) 421 5124.

José Balcarce ★★★

Sublime Andean dishes with a modern twist. Go for a three-course blow-out or just sample a starter like the melt-in-the-mouth llama carpaccio.
Av. Mitre esq. Necochea, Salta. Tel: (0387) 421 1628.

El Rincón de Alejandro ★★★★

Consistently good quality gourmet cuisine served in the rather conservative dining room of this upmarket hotel.
Hotel Alejandro 1. Balcarce 252, Salta. Tel: (0387) 400 0000. www.alejandro1hotel.com.ar

SPORT AND LEISURE

Movitrack

Wide variety of safari trips, to Humahuaca Canyon, Cachi and Cafayate, in excellent customised vehicles, as well as city tours.
Buenos Aires 28, Salta. Tel: (0387) 431 6749. www.movitrack.com.ar

Index

A

accommodation 40–1, 62, 65, 132–5, 160–1, 163–5, 166–8, 169–70, 171, 172
agribusiness 19
air travel 24, 50, 129, 150
airport 129, 150
Alta Gracia 105
Antarctica 121–2
apartamentos 132
Aquarium (Mar del Plata) 39
architecture 35, 103, 107
ArteBA 21
artisanship 44, 111, 118–19
ATMs 150, 152
audio-tours 33
Avenida 9 de Julio (Buenos Aires) 28
Avenida Sarmiento (Mendoza) 93

B

beaches 38–9, 51, 86
beef 136–7
birds 50, 51, 53, 54, 57, 70, 75
boats 53, 55, 64, 70–1, 75, 86, 89, 121, 125, 130, 144–5, 148, 166, 167, 168–9
bodegas 91, 92, 94–5
Borges, Jorge Luis 17
Bosque de Arrayanes 83
Bridges, Lucas 154
Bridges, Thomas 68
Bryn Gwyn field research station 51
Buenos Aires 4, 10–11, 21, 23, 24–5, 26, 27–35, 123–4, 130, 140–1, 142, 145, 146, 149, 160
Buenos Aires region 23, 24, 26–7, 37, 38–41, 44–5, 124–5, 128–9, 163
Buenos Aires Tango Festival 21
buses 128

C

cabanitas 132
Cabecera Sur del Lago Gutiérrez 167–8
cable car 113
Cachi 114
Cafayate 114
cafés 34, 161, 162
Camarones 51
Camino de las Estancias Jesuíticas 101, 102
Canal Beagle 70
canoeing 144–5
canyon-sliding 145
cardon 114

Cariló 38
carnivals 20
Casa del Obispo Mercadillo 103
Casa Rosada 28–9
Cascada Césares 81
cathedrals 103, 113
cave 49, 58–9
Cementerio de Recoleta 34
Central and Southern Patagonia 4, 9, 23, 25, 48–65, 135, 164–6
Central Sierras 9, 101, 105, 108–9
Cerro Aconcagua 9, 98, 120
Cerro Champaquí 9
Cerro Chapelco 89
Cerro Huanquihue 86–7
Cerro Malo 86–7
Cerro San Bernardo 113
Cerro Santa Elena 85
Cerro Torre 60, 61
Cerro Tronador 25, 80
Chacras de Coria 169
chairlift 68–9
children 38, 39, 51, 79, 148–9
churches
  Córdoba 102
  Córdoba region 107
  Salta 113
Círculo Militar 35
climate 126, 127
climbing 60, 87, 98, 120 *see also* walks and hikes
Coctaca 117
coffee 138–9
Colonia del Sacramento 122–3
consulates 159
Convento de San Bernardo 113
Córdoba 100, 102–3, 171
Córdoba region 9, 21, 23, 25, 100–1, 102, 104–9, 171
coypu 56
crafts 44, 111, 118–19, 125, 142, 143
credit cards 160
crime 30, 158–9
cruises 70–1
Cueva de las Manos Pintadas 48, 58–9
culture 16–17, 21, 23, 29, 35, 42, 43, 44, 58–9, 103, 107, 140–1, 162
  see also crafts; gauchos; indigenous peoples; museums and galleries
customs 150
cycling 130, 145

D

dance 16–17, 21, 140–1, 162
Darwin, Charles 71, 72–3
desert 56, 114–15
Día de la Tradición 44–5
disabilities 131, 155
dolphins 57
Don Segundo Sombra (Güiraldes) 42, 44
drives and driving 58, 130, 158
  Central and Southern Patagonia 52–3, 58, 59
  Córdoba region 25, 101, 108–9
  see also tours
drugs 159
duckies 89
duty 150

E

eating out 33, 34, 45, 95, 136, 148–9, 160, 161–2, 165, 167, 168, 170, 171, 172
economy 4, 13, 15, 26, 54, 111, 134–5
ecotourism 144
Edificio Kavanagh 35
El Calafate 62, 165
El Centro (Buenos Aires) 28–9
El Chaltén 60
electricity 150
elephant seal 53, 57
email 150
embassies 159
emergencies 158–9
entertainment 21, 140–1, 149, 162, 165–6, 170
Estancia Alta Gracia 107
Estancia Caroya 106
Estancia Harberton 68
Estancia Jesús María 106–7
Estancia La Candelaria 109
Estancia Peuma Hue 80
Estancia Santa Catalina 107
estancias 23, 25, 40–1, 54, 68, 80, 101, 102–3, 106–7, 108, 109, 132, 134–5, 148, 160, 163–4
Eurocentricity 17, 105
events 20–1, 44–5, 92, 108, 123–4, 146

F

fair trade 119, 143
Falkland Islands 71
fashion 142
fast food 137–8
fauna *see* flora and fauna
Feria de San Pedro Telmo 30

Feria del Libro 21
ferries 64
Festival Nacional de la Doma y el Folklore 21, 108
festivals 21, 44–5, 92, 108
Fiesta Nacional de Cerveza 21
Fiesta Nacional de la Vendimia 21, 92
flora and fauna 46–7, 74, 75, 82–3, 114–15 *see also* wildlife
Florida 34
food and drink 21, 78, 91, 136–9, 143, 148–9 *see also* eating out; wine
football 12, 20–1, 30–1, 36–7, 145
forest 83
4×4 drives 58, 59

G

Gaiman 51
galleries *see* museums and galleries
gardens 32
Garganta del Diablo 80
gauchos 18, 27, 40, 41, 42–3, 44–5, 108, 111, 123–4
geography 8–9
Glaciar Martial 68–9
glaciers 4, 25, 60, 62–3, 68–9, 80
golf 38, 145
guanaco 54
Güemes 118
Guevara, Ernesto (Ché) 104, 105
Güiraldes, Ricardo 42, 44

H

health 152–3, 158
history 10–13, 16–17, 18, 35, 40, 42, 49, 51, 55, 58–9, 67, 68, 69, 71, 72–3, 74–5, 82, 92, 96, 102–3, 104, 105, 106, 111, 112, 154
HMS *Beagle* 71, 72
horse riding 41, 61, 78–9, 99, 105, 146, 170–1
hotels 132–3, 160, 161, 163, 164–5, 166–7, 168, 171
Huacalera 117
Humahuaca 117

I

Iglesia Catedral (Córdoba) 103
Iglesia Catedral (Salta) 113
Iglesia San Francisco 113
Iguazú Falls 4, 23, 46–7
Iguazú Falls region 163–4

Il Caminito (Buenos Aires) 31
Inca people 21, 110, 112, 120–1
indigenous peoples 10, 18–19, 21, 55, 68, 69, 71, 72–3, 74–5, 79, 103, 106, 107, 110, 112, 117, 119, 120–1, 143, 154
insurance 158
internet 150, 155
Inti Raymi 21
Isla Victoria 82–3
Istmo Carlos Ameghino 52

J
Jesuits 23, 25, 101, 102–3, 106–7, 108, 109
Jesús María 108
Junín de los Andes 87

K
kayaking 89, 144–5, 168–9
Kirchner, Néstor 15, 54
kite surfing 88

L
La Boca 30–1
La Bombonera 31, 145
La Cuesta del Obispo 114
La Cumbre 105, 171
La Feria de Mataderos 123–4
Lago Gutiérrez 80
Lago Lácar 86
Lago Mascardi 81
Lago Nahuel Huapi 78, 82–3, 88
Laguna de los Tres 60–1
Laguna del Carbón 54
Laguna Negra 75
Laguna Torre 61
Lake District 23, 25, 76–89, 167–9
land 8–9
land rights 18, 19
language 138, 156–7
Las Islas Malvinas 71
Las Lenas 99
listings 140
literature 17, 21, 42, 44
lodges 169–70
Los Antiguos 59
Los Bosques de Palermo 32–3
love hotels 132, 133

M
Magellanic penguin 57
Malvinas Monument 35
Manzana Jesuítica 102–3
maps 6–7, 22
    Buenos Aires 27
    Buenos Aires region 26
    Central and Southern Patagonia 48, 52
    Córdoba region 100, 109
    Lake District 76, 84

Mendoza region 90, 94
Salta region 110, 116
Tierra del Fuego 66
Mapuche people 19, 79
Mar del Plata 27, 39
mara 56–7
Maradona, Diego 31, 36–7
marine life 23, 49, 50, 51, 52, 53, 54, 55, 57, 70, 71, 122, 148
marine park 54
markets 30, 124, 125
maté 139
Mendoza 21, 92–3, 170
Mendoza region 9, 23, 90–1, 92, 94–5, 96, 97, 98–9, 120–1, 169–71
Menem, Carlos 13, 15
milongas 140, 141
mining 111
money 150, 152, 160
Monumento de los Dos Congresos 28
Moreno, Francisco (Perito) 72, 73, 82
Mount Fitz Roy 60
mountain biking 145
Museo Casa de Ernesto Ché Guevara 105
Museo de Arqueología de Alta Montaña 112
Museo de Arte de Latinoamericano de Buenos Aires 33
Museo de la Casa Rosada 29
Museo de La Patagonia 79
Museo de los Niños Abasto 149
Museo del Área Fundacional 92
Museo del Fin del Mundo 69
Museo Evita 33
Museo Gauchesco Ricardo Güiraldes 44
Museo Histórico del Norte 112
Museo Histórico Nacional Casa del Virrey Liniers 107
Museo Jesuítico Nacional de Jesús María 107
Museo Marítimo y Presidio de Ushuaia 69
Museo Mundo Yámana 69
Museo Municipal (Colonia del Sacramento) 123
Museo Paleontológico Edigio Feruglio 51
Museo Portugués 123
museums and galleries 123
    Buenos Aires 29, 33, 149
    Buenos Aires region 44
    Central and Southern Patagonia 51
    Córdoba region 105, 107

Lake District 79
Mendoza 92
Mendoza region 95
Salta 112
Tierra del Fuego 67, 69, 149
music 16–17, 21, 140–1, 162, 170
Myba Guaraní people 19
myrtle forest 83

N
national parks 46–7
    Central and Southern Patagonia 4, 23, 25, 49, 54–5, 59, 60, 62–5
    Lake District 82–3, 86–7
    Salta region 114–15
    Tierra del Fuego 68–9, 74–5
nightlife 140, 165–6, 170

O
opening hours 152

P
Palacio Congreso 28
Palermo 32–3
Paleta de Pintor 117
pampas 23, 24, 40–1, 163
paragliding 88, 105
parks
    Buenos Aires 32
    Mendoza 93
    Mendoza region 98
    Salta 113
    see also national parks
Parque General San Martín (Mendoza) 93
Parque Nacional Iguazú 46–7
Parque Nacional Lanín 86–7
Parque Nacional Los Alerces 59
Parque Nacional Los Cardones 114–15
Parque Nacional Los Glaciares 60
Parque Nacional Monte León 54–5
Parque Nacional Nahuel Huapi 82–3
Parque Nacional Perito Moreno 59
Parque Nacional Tierra del Fuego 68–9, 74–5
Parque Nacional Torres del Paine 23, 25, 49, 64–5
Parque Provincial Aconcagua 98
Parque San Martín (Salta) 113
passports 123, 152
Patagonia 72–3 see also Central and Southern Patagonia; Tierra del Fuego

Paz, José Clemente 34, 35
penguins 50, 51, 57
Península Quertrihué 83
Península San Pedro 78
Península Valdés 23, 25, 50–1, 52–3
Perito Moreno 59
Perito Moreno glacier 4, 25, 62–3
Perón, Eva 12, 14, 33, 34
Perón, Isabel 15
Perón, Juan 12, 14–15
pharmacies 152–3
phones 153
Pinamar 39
Planetario Galileo Galilei 32–3
Playa Catritre 86
Playa Elola 51
Plaza de Chacras de Coria (Mendoza) 93
Plaza de Congreso (Buenos Aires) 28
Plaza de Mayo (Buenos Aires) 28–9
Plaza General San Martín (Mendoza) 92–3
Plaza Independencia (Mendoza) 92–3
Plaza Julio Cortázar (Buenos Aires) 32
Plaza 9 de Julio (Salta) 112
Plaza San Martín (Buenos Aires) 34, 35
Plaza San Martín (Córdoba) 103
Poincenot 60–1
police 158, 159
politics 4, 11, 12, 13, 14–15, 19, 28
polo 146, 162–3
ponchos 118
post 153
prehistoric remains 49, 51, 58–9, 112
public holidays 21, 153–4
public transport 47, 74, 113, 125, 128–9
Pucará de Tilcara 117
pudu 57
Puente del Inca 98, 120–1
Puerto de Frutas 125
Puerto Madero 28, 29
Puerto Madryn 50–1, 165–6
Puerto Pirámides 52
Puerto San Julián 55
Punta Arenas 64
Punta Delgada 53
Punta Norte 53
Punta Tombo 51
Purmamarca 117

Q
Quebrada de Cafayate 115
Quebrada de Humahuaca 116–17

R

rafting 84–5, 88–9, 99, 170–1
reading 154
religion 102–3, 106, 107
Reserva Ecológica Costanera Sur 29
restaurants 136, 148–9, 161–2, 165, 167, 170, 171, 172
Retiro 34–5
Río Manso 81, 84–5
Río Mendoza 99
Río Paraná 124–5
Río Uruguay 124–5
Roca, General Julio 18
Ruiz de Arellano Plaza (San Antonio de Areco) 45
Ruta 40 58, 114
Ruta de Siete Lagos 87

S

safety 30, 65, 85, 98, 115, 158
Salta 112–13, 172
Salta region 23, 25, 110–11, 114–18, 172
San Antonio de Areco 44–5, 163
San Carlos de Bariloche 76, 78–9, 169
San Martín, José de 11
San Martín de los Andes 76, 86–7
San Salvador de Jujuy 116–17
San Telmo 30
Santa Cruz coast 54–5

sea lions 53
seals 53, 57
seasons 126–7
ships 70–1, 121
shopping 30, 33, 119, 124, 125, 142–3
silver trade 111
skiing 60, 69, 77, 89, 99, 146–7
smoking 140
snowboarding 89, 146–7
solar clock 117
southern right whale 52, 53, 57
spas 147
sponsorship of children 149
sport and activities 12, 20–1, 23, 30–1, 36–7, 38, 39, 41, 60, 61, 64, 69, 75, 77, 78–9, 80, 88–9, 91, 98, 99, 105, 144–7, 162–3, 166, 168–9, 170–1 *see also* climbing; water sports
steppe 9

T

tango 16–17, 21, 140–1, 162
tax 143, 150, 154
taxis 131
Teatro Colón 29
Tehuelche people 55
telos 132, 133
theatre 29
Tierra del Fuego 23, 25, 66–71, 72–3, 74–5, 149,

166–7
Tigre 124–5
Tilcara 117
time differences 154–5
tipping 136
toilets 155
tourist information 65, 102, 129, 155
tours 4–5, 46–7, 121–2
  Buenos Aires 33
  Buenos Aires region 45, 125
  Central and Southern Patagonia 63
  Córdoba region 102
  Lake District 78–9, 84–5, 86, 87
  Mendoza region 91, 92, 94–5, 98–9
  Salta 113
  Salta region 114–17
  Tierra del Fuego 70–1 *see also* drives and driving
trains 47, 74, 113, 125, 128–9
transport 24, 50, 128–31, 145, 150 *see also* boats; drives and driving; horse riding; public transport
Trelew 50, 51

U

universities 102
Ushuaia 25, 67, 68–9, 121, 149, 166–7
Uspallata 120

V

vaccinations 158
Ventisquero Negro 80
Villa Fiorito 37
Villa La Angostura 83
Villa Quila Quina 86
Villas Miserias 39
visas 123, 152
Volcán Lanín 87

W

walks and hikes 23, 25, 147, 168–9, 170–1
  Central and Southern Patagonia 60–1, 63, 65
  Lake District 86–7
  Mendoza region 98, 120–1
  Tierra del Fuego 75
water sports 81, 84–5, 88–9, 99, 144–5, 170–1 *see also* boats
waterfalls 4, 23, 46–7, 81
weather 126, 127
websites 155
whales 52, 53, 57
Wichi people 119
wildlife 25, 50, 54, 56–7 *see also* marine life
wind surfing 88
wine 21, 23, 91, 92, 94–7, 114, 138, 143, 169–70
woods 32

Y

Yámana people 69, 71, 74–5

Acknowledgements

The publishers would like to thank the following individuals and organisations for providing their copyright photographs for this book:

EXTREMO SUR page 85
FLICKR.COM pages 151 (Antonio García), 17 (Gisela Giardino) & 101 (Facundo A Fernández)
MARION MORRISON page 21
MIKE JOHNSON pages 45, 118, 119
GETTY IMAGES pages 36 & 37
WIKIMEDIA COMMONS pages 13 (taken in 1972), 57 (Michaël Catanzariti), 72, 73 (Miguel A Monjas), 121 (Eurico Zimbres), 122 (Andrew Mandem), 125 (Facundo A Fernández), 138 (Paul Keller) & 155
WORLD PICTURES/PHOTOSHOT pages 1 & 42
All the rest Jane Egginton and Iain MacIntyre

Copy-editing: JOANNE OSBORNE for CAMBRIDGE PUBLISHING MANAGEMENT LTD

Proofreading: PENNY ISAAC for CAMBRIDGE PUBLISHING MANAGEMENT LTD

SEND YOUR THOUGHTS TO
BOOKS@THOMASCOOK.COM

We're committed to providing the very best up-to-date information in our travel guides and constantly strive to make them as useful as they can be. You can help us to improve future editions by letting us have your feedback. If you've made a wonderful discovery on your travels that we don't already feature, if you'd like to inform us about recent changes to anything that we do include, or if you simply want to let us know your thoughts about this guidebook and how we can make it even better – we'd love to hear from you.

Send us ideas, discoveries and recommendations today and then look out for your valuable input in the next edition of this title.

Emails to the above address, or letters to Travellers Project Editor, Thomas Cook Publishing, PO Box 227, Coningsby Road, Peterborough PE3 8SB, UK.

Please don't forget to let us know which title your feedback refers to!